Helion & Company Limited
Unit 8 Amherst Business Centre
Budbrooke Road
Warwick
CV34 5WE
England
Tel. 01926 499 619
Email: info@helion.co.uk
Website: www.helion.co.uk
Twitter: @helionbooks
Visit our blog https://helionbooks.wordpress.com/

Typeset by Oliver Barstow, Milan, Italy
Cover design by Paul Hewitt, Battlefield Design (www.battlefield-design.co.uk)

ISBN 978-1-804513-76-7

British Library Cataloguing-in-Publication Data
A catalogue record for this book is available from the British Library

CONTENTS

Note: In order to simplify the use of this book, all names, locations and geographic designations are as provided in *The Times World Atlas*, or other traditionally accepted major sources of reference, as of the time of described events.

ACRONYMS AND ABBREVIATIONS

AAA anti-aircraft artillery
AAC Army Air Corps, US (also see USAAC)
AAF Army Air Forces
AAFBU Army Air Force Base Unit
ACC Air Coordinating Committee
ACTS Air Corps Tactical School
ADC Air Defense Command
AEC Atomic Energy Commission
AF Air Force (as in Eighth AF)
AFB Air Force Base
AFSWP Armed Forces Special Weapons Project
APC Air Policy Commission (Finletter Commission)
AWPD Air War Plans Division
BW Bombardment Wing
CAF Continental Air Forces
CAPB Congressional Aviation Policy Board
CEP Circular Error Probability (or Probable)
CPFF Cost-Plus-Fixed-Fee
CVA US Navy attack aircraft carrier
FG Fighter Group
ft feet
GDP Gross Domestic Product
JCS Joint Chiefs of Staff
JPS Joint Staff Planners
JSPC Joint Strategic Plans Committee
JWPC Joint War Plans Committee
km kilometres
KT kiloton of explosive yield
m metres
MATS Military Air Transport Service
NAA North American Aviation
NACA National Advisory Committee for Aeronautics
NSS National Storage Sites
PVO *Protivo Vosdushnaya Oborono Strany* (Soviet Air Defence Forces)
RAF Royal Air Force
RBS Radar Bomb Scoring
RFC Reconstruction Financing Corporation
SAC Strategic Air Command
TAC Tactical Air Command
UAC United Aircraft Corporation
UATC United Aircraft and Transport Corporation
UK United Kingdom
UN United Nations
USAAC United States Army Air Corps
USAAF United States Army Air Forces
USAAS United States Army Air Service
USS United States Ship
USSR Union of Soviet Socialist Republics
WSEG Weapons System Evaluation Group

PREFACE

This is the second in a series of 15 volumes telling the story of land-based and seaborne American air power between 1945 and 1990, divided into five separate chronological periods, each span of time served with three volumes dedicated respectively to covering US fighters, bombers and naval combat aircraft. It also covers the development of how the industry changed and adapted, how tactical and strategic policy planning evolved, how design and manufacturing trends kept pace with new technology and in what way the Air Force and the Navy accommodated political and military objectives.

This volume is in two separate books. This one, *Volume 2 Part 1*, covers the way possession of the atomic bomb influenced not only US strategy but also defence policy at a geopolitical level, relying on this weapon to underpin a concept of total response to unprovoked aggression while restraining financial commitments to national security. It also covers specific war plans and debate over the possibility of carrying out a pre-emptive strike on the Soviet Union, concluding with the first few years of Strategic Air Command and the background story to the bomber manufacturers of the time.

The second book, *Volume 2 Part 2*, covers bomber development, technology and a detailed look at the aircraft which kept the atomic force up and running between 1945 and 1949, together with descriptions of prototypes and experimental aircraft designs which failed to make it into production and which never served with the Air Force.

Their purpose is to tell the story of air power and to set the aircraft within the context of national and international events, changing patterns of political and programmatic decisions and the way technology opened new opportunities for industry and how research led to new manufacturing possibilities and operational capabilities. Central to each volume, however, is the integrated story of the airframes and the engines which defined possibilities and how those were filtered into separate applications and the most successful used in the Air Force and the Navy.

Within the practical confines of each volume it is not possible to tell the full story of each aircraft type, either those placed in production or tested without successful service use, and many types were operational across several of these five chronological periods. Where service use spans successive volumes, the initial coverage tells the story of that type's origin and early development picking up the story as the series progresses, covering the conflicts in which they took part.

Volume 3 will complete this first period of 1945–1949 with coverage of US naval aviation in a similar format and with the same layout, covering legacy types from the Second World War and the emerging age of jet-powered fighters and attack aircraft. Successive volumes will cover Air Force fighters and bombers and naval combat aircraft in the Korean War (1950–1953), before moving to the period during which the century-series appeared and supersonic combat aircraft became operational (1954–1960). The series then moves to the period when much change occurred before and during the Vietnam War (1961–1975) before covering the closing years of the Cold War when stealth and advanced combat systems were introduced (1976–1990).

Operational histories will be introduced only when they pertain to the development of fighter and bomber aircraft of the periods covered, emphasis being placed instead on the technical and engineering development of the different aircraft types. There are already copious sources for readers to obtain highly detailed accounts of operational histories. As with this first book, successive volumes will also include failed types either proposed and never built or brought to experimental evaluation without series production.

I wanted to write this series because I felt that the story of American air power had usually been defined through either the type histories of aircraft involved or the personal reminiscences of pilots and aircrew. Nowhere was there a single source of reference that brought it all together, with coverage of the aviation industry, the political base upon which significant decisions were made and the technical choices available to manufacturers and design teams. By integrating the story of these aspects with the aircraft in general, I wanted to provide something different, through coverage that also included the technical, engineering, industrial, political and strategic decisions that both shaped the US Air Force and the US Navy and the way they evolved throughout the Cold War.

David Baker
England, 2024

INTRODUCTION

As defined through the experiences of air power leaders in the Second World War, by the acceptance in the general public that it was the dominant factor in modern warfare and in the practical demonstration of its capabilities, strategic bombing was at the forefront of planning for a post-war Air Force. A time in which the long-range bomber carrying atomic weapons was at the core of deterrence, rapidly seen as the key to preventing another global conflict. With the added complexity of a strategy aimed at a single potential enemy, decisions and judgements about air power levels and capabilities were made on the basis of the assessed threat from the Soviet Union.

With the introduction of the jet engine into combat aircraft, higher performance levels challenged design teams to find ways to best fit the new technology to existing airframes and that brought problems causing delays. For the 1945–1949 period, only the North American B-45 Tornado provided experience with operating and maintaining jet bombers while the B-47 was similarly delayed but largely because of new and innovative features such as the laminar-flow, swept-back wing with underslung engine pods and unconventional placement of the landing gear. Finding solutions to technical challenges such as these, in addition to integrating advanced electronic and flight control systems prevented the B-47 from entering service before the start of the Korean War, a story picked up in *Volume 5: Bombers 1950–1953*.

For much of this period, the strategic atomic deterrent was carried by piston-engine bombers such as the B-29 and the B-50. The B-36 would serve as a transition type when it acquired supplementary propulsion from four J47 turbojet engines carried under the wings. Largely ignored as a mere tweaking of the B-29, the B-50 was the first US bomber designed to carry atomic weapons and while it bore strong visual resemblance to its precursor, two-thirds of it was completely different to the B-29. That alone raises it from obscurity as one of the most important aircraft of the interwar period between 1945 and 1949.

1
AIR POLICY AND THE STRATEGIC BOMBER

On 15 October 1949, a nationwide Gallup Poll asked the American public a single question of profound significance for public perception of the US military: 'If the United States should get into another World War, which branch of the armed forces do you think would play the most important part in winning the war – the Army, the Navy or the Air Force?'

Of those responding, 74 percent of Americans put their faith in the Air Force, six percent in the Army and four percent in the Navy; as many as 16 percent placed responsibility in other government departments, expecting diplomacy or the secret service to keep them safe. But the message was clear. The majority of Americans looked to the air for engaging with and defeating future enemies. The results surprised some, particularly those who had served in the Second World War and fought on land or at sea and believed their affiliated service to have done the most to win that conflict. It shocked the Army and the Navy who had been fighting a long and bitter inter-service rivalry for pre-eminence and legislative priority, both in Congress and the White House.

Two years earlier, on 18 September 1947, the US National Security Act made the Air Force independent as an autonomous arm of the newly created Department of Defense. Rivalry had been there when the Air Forces operated under Army aegis but since separation in 1947, the Air Force had been regarded by the Army as nothing more than an adjunct to mainstream military operations for tactical support. But the Navy had used air power to engage with and to defeat the land, sea and air forces of Imperial Japan and fought hard to present its carrier-borne strike capability as the foundation for strategic defence of the United States.

The policies of the US government under President Harry S Truman would shape planning for air power compromised by demobilisation and a reduction in men and materiel as the White House pursued a balancing of the books at the expense of defence. (Harry S Truman Library)

George F Kennan, one of the so-called four 'Wise Men', shaped foreign policy and a concept of containment, proselytising the concept of all-out response to Soviet military aggression. (Author archive)

When President Truman signed the National Security Act in 1947 he appointed General Carl A Spaatz to lead the independent Air Force and directed the first Secretary of Defense James H Forrestal to end inter-service bickering and backbiting in the interests of national security, thus ensuring a proper configuration of those new responsibilities managed through the Pentagon. But it was asking too much and there was little cooperation between the three armed services with high levels of acrimony each directed at the other two. There was even disagreement over the respective roles and responsibilities each service would administer.

Any decision over the strategic responsibilities of the respective armed services had to take account of national means and resources, as well as the threats faced by the United States in its new-found role as the world's largest military power. Disputes like these frustrated the political leadership faced with aggressive and brutish messages emanating from the Soviet Union, where Josef Stalin and the Kremlin leadership presided over a vast expanse of Eastern Europe which Russian soldiers occupied at the end of the Second World War.

As early as 1946, the intentions of the USSR had been made clear in a speech delivered by Stalin on 9 February when he declared that the unprecedented expansion of industrialisation to support the war effort would continue unabated in the post-war period. This, he said, was to combat the unexpurgated causes of war which he attributed to capitalist imperialism and territorial hegemony from anti-socialist countries. Under-Secretary of State Dean Acheson characterised it is as defining 'with brutal clarity the Soviet Union's post-war policy'.

Kennan's book *Russia and the West* was a 'must-read', displayed here on the desk of F P Callaghan with R Ruth Carey at the Atomic Energy Commission, the body responsible for controlling production of atomic weapons. (NARA)

Unlike his predecessor Franklin D Roosevelt, who had succumbed to long-term illness on 12 April 1945, President Truman was cautious about trusting Stalin and pledges he made at the Potsdam conference later that year to allow free elections in East European countries. Moreover, Truman was determined to contain communism behind its existing borders and toward that objective formulated what became known as the Truman Doctrine on 12 March 1947, bolstered on 4 July 1948 when he approved support for the fight for democracy in Greece and Turkey.

In addition, on 3 April 1948 the US Congress enacted Truman's Marshall Plan, laid out by General George C Marshall, allocating financial aid for the impoverished countries of Western Europe. Director of Policy Planning at the Department of States, George Kennan articulated the Truman Doctrine as a policy of 'containment' and defined the 'domino-effect' whereby the fall of one country to communism could induce a ripple effect elsewhere.

While balancing the needs of the domestic economy and building diplomatic ties with democratic governments and friendly countries, Truman presided over a period of demobilisation and contraction in the armed services, reducing its manpower from 12 million in June 1945 to little more than 1.5 million men and women two years later. In 1947 the Army had 683,000 personnel, the Navy 484,000 and the Air Force fewer than 306,000 while the Marine Corps had 92,000. From a wartime maximum of 218 groups, when the Air Force became independent in 1947 that number stood at 38 of which only 11 were fully operational. None of the nine B-29 groups were fully manned.

It was the same for the other services. From 91 ground divisions on VJ-Day, in mid-1947 the Army had only 10 divisions on strength while the Marine Corps had been reduced from six divisions to two. At its maximum strength during wartime the Navy had 8,165 vessels of all types including 1,304 major combat ships, of which 40 were aircraft carriers and 24 were battleships. By mid-1947 the Navy possessed a fleet of only 1,003 ships of which 289 were major combat types including 14 carriers and four battleships.

Placing priority on the restoration of a peacetime economy based around production and manufacturing for a domestic market and with great export potential to a war-torn world, the Truman administration sought to balance a drastically reduced defence budget against an increasingly challenging range of international threats to national security. In this two-year period after the Second World War, several approaches were mooted as ways of providing adequate national defence while constraining government expenditure.

As early as 1945 Truman proposed to substitute selective military service with one year of universal military training involving all men aged 18 years or on graduating from High School. On completion of training they would become members of the general reserve in a programme not dissimilar to National Service in the UK. Fearing an electoral backlash, Congress batted it away and it was never discussed but a commission appointed on 19 December 1946 and led by Dr Carl Compton looked at it again and issued a report on 29 May 1947. Fearing accusations of 'militarism', Congress turned to the then-impending National Security Act establishing the Department of Defense as a reason not to discuss it, believing that adequate military force would be obtained through the career programme for serving officers and men.

But the Joint Chiefs of Staff (JCS) were worried that the Soviet Union retained a large, numerically superior standing army. They believed that in any future war the United States would not have the advantage of allies holding the line while it mobilised for conflict, as it had in the Second World War when Britain and its Commonwealth stood alone for more than two years after declaring war on Germany. What concerned the JCS most was the military power of the Soviet Union as a threat to peace in Western Europe, the reason why it had gone to war in 1917 and why it had adopted a 'Europe first' policy in December 1941 when Japan attacked Pearl Harbor.

Collectively, the US military intelligence community concluded that the Russians still had 4.7 million men under arms of which 3.8 million were ground forces, 650,000 were in the air force and 300,000 in their navy. Combat units filled 150 divisions while the air force had 89,000 aircraft of all types, although almost all of it tactical with large numbers being redundant or semi-operational. Their strategic bomber force was almost non-existent and the navy had around 150 vessels, of which four were old battleships supported by nine cruisers, 55 destroyers, 132 submarines and no carriers. They had no blue-water, ocean-going force and no means of projecting power beyond the limits of their standing army.

Black USAAC cadets learning basic flying skills before going on to segregated trades in the US Army Air Corps. (USAF)

Seeking Direction

Two years before the National Security Act of 1947, the Air Forces then operating under the US Army, based future force requirements at 78 groups and at least 638,000 men. At the War Department, General Marshall had wanted a post-war force of only 16 groups and 120,000 airmen. But that was considered unreasonable and in December 1945 the force level was set at a maximum 70 groups incorporating 26 bomber groups and 25 fighter groups. As will be discussed later, that was harder to achieve than stated. But implicit in the National Security Act was Executive Order 9877, also signed by President Truman on 26 July 1947, in which the roles of the armed services were defined with greater clarity than within the Act.

It responded specifically to the insistence by several members of Congress that the Navy retain its air capability in a written definition that went further than similar mandates for the Army or the Air Force. The Air Force was required to gain and maintain air superiority, establish local command of the air as required, to provide airborne support operations, conduct strategic warfare and to support land and sea forces as needed. The Army was to seize and control land areas through joint amphibious and airborne operations.

The role of the Navy was to include control of key sea lanes and protect them from incursions, to attack and constrain enemy sea communications, support occupation forces with Marine units, conduct naval reconnaissance, carry out anti-submarine warfare, protect shipping and seize shore positions to neutralise enemy occupation or action. The Act itself had set out the importance of naval aviation which was seen by the Navy as implicit in their mandate. The potential and inevitable rise and application of the carrier task group was seen as a flagship force supplanting the battleship as the capital ship of the fleet.

Truman was determined not to make the mistakes of 1919, where a lack of support for a peacetime air force allowed the industry and America's application of that as an effective instrument for national security to fall behind developments in other countries, especially Europe and Britain. On 8 August 1945 he wrote to John Snyder at the Office of Mobilization and Conversion raising 'concern for the future of the aircraft industry'. In searching for a way to structure a policy in which the air force and its supporting industry could be held at a greater state of readiness, Truman turned to the Morrow Report of 1925 for guidance and to seek lessons as to why that had not been achieved after the First World War.

Headed by Dwight D Morrow, it had been tasked with finding the 'best means of developing and applying aircraft in national defense', concluding that the Army Air Service should be renamed the Army Air Corps, that it should receive two brigadier-generals as assistant chiefs and that it should receive a five-year expansion programme. Congress enacted the formation of the Army Air Corps on 2 July 1926 but funds were never allocated for the expansion programme. In fact, the Morrow Report was not as far-seeing as the Lassiter Board of 1923, which recommended a force of bomber and pursuit types for conducting independent missions, or the Lampert Committee established by the House of Representatives in 1925 which called for an independent air force.

The independent evaluation of post-war air power requirements pre-dated the Truman presidency. It began when the acting Secretary of State Joseph C Grew, Secretary of War Stimson, Secretary of the Navy Forrestal and Secretary of Commerce Henry A Wallace signed a joint memorandum on 27 March 1945 setting up the Air Coordinating Committee (ACC). It comprised representatives of the Army Air Forces (AAF), the Civil Aeronautics Board and other interested government departments and although it had no statutory power to enforce recommendations, on 19 September 1946 Truman signed Executive Order 9781 giving it full authority to 'develop and recommend integrated policies to be carried out and actions to be taken by the participating agencies or by any other government agency charged with responsibility in the aviation field'.

Much of the work conducted by the ACC was so embroiled by the post-war demobilisation and contraction of defence forces that it had little opportunity for its primary mandate, crafting a peacetime air policy. Nevertheless, it provided the basis upon which future groups would rely for writing such recommendations for an autonomous air force. That began when the ACC's chairman Garrison Norton wrote to Truman on 16 June 1947 imparting information about the American aircraft industry, proposing that he authorise a board of impartial citizens to study the relationship between it and national security. The following day, Truman responded by acquiescing and confirming to Norton that he had appointed an Air Policy Commission (APC) to do just that.

Truman's rapid response to Norton's plea had been timely. Concerned at the deterioration in the state of the post-war aviation industry and putting faith in the ACC, he also wanted to get ahead of a separate enquiry board being planned by the opposition Republican Party in Congress. That emerged on 22 July 1947 as the Congressional Aviation Policy Board (CAPB), approved by the President on 30 July, which held its first meeting on 15 September. However, and perhaps ironically, it was the APC that held the greatest weight, although both that and the CAPB interviewed almost exactly the same people, simply because it was a President's commission and in the nuances of government hierarchy that raised it both intellectually and in significance.

The first US Secretary of Defense, James V Forrestal is sworn in on 17 September 1947 but lacking political experience he would be pressured to resign just 18 months later and would commit suicide after suffering from depression. (The White House)

Predating the restoration of peace, Secretary of State Joseph C Grew had been a principal architect of the Air Coordinating Committee which would define the shape of post-war policy for both civil and military aviation. (NARA)

Truman selected the members of the APC with great care and consideration for their importance and the respective contributions they brought to the task, asking Thomas K Finletter to be the chairman of the commission. Finletter had served in the Army where he reached the rank of captain, practised law since 1930 and had overseen legal aspects of US military aircraft sold to France

Demobilisation compromised preparation for a standoff against the Soviet Union which influenced the political leadership to use the atomic monopoly as a leverage against depleted manpower levels. (NARA)

before the Second World War when he held several senior positions with the government. Highly respected for his objectively balanced views, he brought honesty and integrity with a reputation for organisational skills.

Vice Chairman of the commission, George P Baker had majored in history, economics and government and at the time of his appointment was a professor of transportation studies at Harvard University after serving with the State Department. During the war, as a colonel he had served on General Arnold's staff managing industrial mobilisation. Newspaper publisher Palmer Hoyt was the third member of the Finletter Commission and brought a knowledge of aviation together with the ideal balance between an understanding of public expectations and the needs of the country. Arthur D Whiteside was a financial and business adviser capable of providing both economic and industrial guidance, while Henry Ford II came on as the fourth member. Ford resigned and was replaced on 27 September 1947 by the engineer John A McCone who owned an iron works.

The APC, better known to historians as the Finletter Commission, was sworn in at the Commerce Department on 29 July 1947 and, with a mandate to deliver its judgements on US air policy by 1 January 1948, it had to move quickly. Both the Finletter Commission and the CAPB shared the same demonstration of tactical naval air activity at sea aboard the USS *Midway* on 21 October and the APC had a full diary as they toured manufacturing facilities across the country. Impressed by the degree of public interest in its activity, the commission held formal hearings between 8 September and 3 December and in all conducted 206 formal sessions for their report.

In collating existing material as reference, the commission assembled a vast library of documents, reports and transcripts of related hearings and assembled the records of their own hearings filling 4,000 pages in six bound volumes. Issues surrounding defence and national security dominated its work as this was the central focus of uncertainty within the industry, across the armed services and among the public, concerned at the level of contraction in the military equipment and personnel and alarmed at the diminishing budgets for the freshly minted Department of Defense.

Commission hearings occurred right at the time the National Security Act was giving the Air Force uncertain autonomy and while commercial issues loomed large, the underpinning conclusion was

General Douglas MacArthur signs the Japanese surrender on 2 September 1945 on the USS *Missouri* in Tokyo Bay, bringing the war in the Pacific to a close far ahead of the anticipated date. (US Navy)

the vulnerability of military capabilities in an unpredictable world and in a national defence force with an uncertain future. The overriding consensus declared strategic air power and the associated doctrine of strategic bombing to be the binding spine of national air power and force projection, enabled through a 70-group Air Force, although the Navy was fighting its own campaign to take that responsibility away from the Air Force and place it on its carrier forces.

In testimony before the commission, on 11 November General Dwight D Eisenhower declared that 'I firmly believe that a reasonably balanced Air Force is one of the greatest assurances we have that we will be respected elsewhere in the world', adding that 'you cannot be militarily strong without a strong Air Force. You cannot beat a strong Air Force'. When asked about that, General Douglas MacArthur opined that he favoured 'an Atomic Striking Force, under a single commander, capable of destroying at least the fifty most important targets in USSR in a single day'. While accepting the doctrine of massive strategic retaliation for any unprovoked attack by another country, Admiral Chester Nimitz reminded the commission that it was essential to see that 'our carrier task forces and out shore-based naval aviation units are equipped and trained to make the best use of all new weapon development of the future'.

Reinforcing concerns expressed by the Navy that the Air Force was considered the *de-facto* custodian of strategic nuclear retaliation, the former Assistant Secretary of the Navy for Air, Artemus Lamb Gates declared that he had 'become more and more concerned over the emphasis that has been placed on the requirements of the United States Air Force and because of this emphasis that the public will overlook the problem of naval aviation or will be inclined to minimise these problems', claiming that in his view the 'backbone of the Navy is its aviation…there is no question in my mind that

The B-29 remained the immediate asset for strategic bombing after the Second World War, the front aircraft here being a B-29-45-BW (42-24727) which was delivered to the 873rd BS of the 498th BG on 18 December 1944. (USAF)

the striking power of the carrier task group is one of the strongest offensive roles we have in air power today', finally that he hoped 'the public and the Congress would not get in the frame of thinking that the Air Force is completely responsible for the development of aviation'.

Finletter Policy

In retrospect and scrutinising the testimony at public and closed hearings, it is difficult today not to find the commission predisposed to favouring the Air Force. It had, after all, been set up in the third quarter of 1947 when the Air Force became independent of the Army, and its liaison officer to the commission was emphatic about expectations when he expressed a belief that it would, surely:

> develop a report to the President which will have far reaching effects upon the Air Force. The future Air Force may depend heavily upon the recommendations of the commission. It is essential that the Air Force pursue this activity to the end that there should be accomplished the satisfactory development of policies which are in the interests of the Air Force.

It could be said that the Navy provided personal testimony while the Air Force issued a directive. However veiled that may have been in the guise of a briefing paper, the 'instruction' to the commission had an inevitability about it. During hearings, seminal presentations were delivered by General Carl Spaatz, the Air Force Chief of Staff, and by Stuart Symington, the Secretary of the Air Force, both of whom appeared on 17 November. Each testified that a 70-group Air Force was the minimum required for national security but warned that because of budget cuts only 55 operational groups could be fielded by 1 January 1948. Finletter was shocked to learn of this, declaring that 'It seems to me an extremely serious statement. It means anything less than that leaves the country in an insecure condition', to which Spaatz wholeheartedly concurred.

Symington claimed the Air Force needed 6,869 aircraft to fill the 70 groups with 3,212 for the Air National Guard and 2,360 for the Air Reserve. To maintain a fully efficient force, production of 3,200 aircraft per year was required which called upon industry to deliver 46.4 million pounds (21 million kg) of airframes. But he also cautioned that under present budgets the Air Force could never reach more than 55 groups and would eventually fall to less than 40 groups on projected budgets, while testifying to the commission that 70 groups was essential to 'undertake immediate and powerful retaliation – a capacity which is itself the only real deterrent to aggression in the world today'.

When asked about the Truman defence budget cap of $11 billion, Secretary of Defense Forrestal explained that 'we are keeping our military expenditures below the levels which our military leaders must in good conscience estimate as the minimum which would themselves ensure national security. By doing so we are able to increase our expenditures to assist in European security'. He claimed that this was acceptable as, in his view, the United States had a significant advantage in weapons. This disclosure would install a suspicion on the part of many politicians that they were asking their taxpayers to restore economic prosperity to post-war European countries.

The Finletter hearings closed on 3 December 1947 with an unambiguous understanding that 70 groups were essential for adequate security, asserting that naval aviation would never equal the capacity of the Air Force for strategic deterrence, and that strategic strike power was a central pillar of national defence. When it was submitted, the final report was both apocalyptic and uncompromising, assessing that the United States was in mortal danger from multiple threats that could be eliminated 'only if the institution of war itself is abolished under law', that it called for 'a force in being in peacetime greater than any self-governing people has ever kept'. Success in war could only be achieved, it said, by 'meeting the attack when it comes but, even more important, capable of dealing a crushing counteroffensive blow on the aggressor'.

On Wednesday, 14 January 1948, the Finletter Commission presented a leather-bound copy of its report to the President. Bearing the title *Survival in the Air War*, in 182 pages it first defined the nature of warfare in the second half of the century, projecting the possibility of guided missiles within 10–25 years, stipulated a minimum 70 groups for the Air Force and projected a national defence budget increase from just under $14 billion in 1949 to $18 billion by 1952. Over those three years, funds for the Air Force alone would be required to rise considerably while those for the Navy were required to increase so that the annual procurement of aircraft could grow larger.

A second major section in the report addressed the current state of the industry, its health, strengths and weaknesses, citing what was necessary for it to match the rising demands of growth in the military sector while accommodating the requirements for a burgeoning commercial market. Broadened out to addressing the National Military Establishment (generally referred to as the NME) across industry, taking in to a greater degree the entire economic and manufacturing base across the nation, it concluded that this must not be dismembered if the United States was to make the best use of existing resources built up across several years of conflict during the Second World War.

The third part of the report focused on research and development, painstakingly pointing out that a threat to US pre-eminence in aeronautics was already posed by Britain which, 'in spite of a generally strained economy has made drastic sacrifices' for air research. It cited development there of new, post-war facilities including the National Gas Turbine establishment at Whetstone, the new Aeronautical Research Centre at Bedford and the new Telecommunications Establishment at Malvern. The report also noted the resurgence of a national aeronautics industry in France and the general resurgence of a technological base to post-war developments.

Almost a quarter of the report was consigned to a discussion of civil aviation in all its varied forms including commercial activities, the involvement of the government in regulation, taxation and constraints on monopolies, together with the national need for more airports, air safety and the national air traffic control and management systems which were expected to grow exponentially. The fifth part of the report was concerned with government organisation and legislation, control of industries vital to the national economy and to the wellbeing of its vital assets. In all, a comprehensive overview of the state of the aviation sector as a vibrant component of the American economy, integrating both civil and military assets, benefits and national rewards, be they for monetary gain or national defence.

In a classified attachment to the official report, the commission drew the President's attention to interventions from James E Webb, Director of the Bureau of the Budget (BoB) and the forerunner to the Office of Management and Budget (OMB) which it became in 1970. Webb was highly sceptical of fiscal demands from the military and the commission was concerned that he had exerted 'a growing tendency…to establish advance estimates of budget requirements of the services and to present these…as ceiling figures which they cannot exceed', ignoring, they said 'the strategic needs of the services', claiming that 'no agency of Government should be empowered to impose fund limitations in a manner now being exercised'. This was not an unexpected ploy from Webb. Since he became director of the BoB in July 1946, Webb had maintained a close working relationship with Truman and was cognisant of his desire for fiscal constraint.

As noted previously, Truman was adamant about keeping the national finances in check and preventing the possibility of a recession as the country adapted to a peacetime economy. On the negative side, there was already some concern about the post-war national budget balance. In 1948 federal government receipts totalled $55.7 billion, largely flat-lining at this level for the next three years, against which it spent $44 billion in 1948 and $55.5 billion in 1949, outlays marginally exceeding income in 1950. In 1948 the government spent only 17 percent of Gross Domestic Product (GDP), rising to 20.5 percent in 1949 and 22.7 percent in 1950. It was against this struggle for fiscal prudence that the Department of Defense fought for higher funds which the Finletter Commission expressed as a vital, national need. In 1948 the government spent 31 percent of its budget on defence, 34 percent in 1949 and just under 30 percent in 1950.

Somewhat disingenuously, while admitting that the programme it recommended would cost the taxpayer a lot of money, the Commission noted that since 1915, 85 percent of federal expenditure had gone on 'war or preparation or payment for war', while asserting that 'the expenditures which we recommend, however, would be small in comparison with the cost of another war'. Aware that the report would be read by the general public if they chose to do so, it used a reassuring tone when declaring that it had not rushed to rash conclusions, basing its determinations on a 'critical analysis' and expressing the incontestable truth that 'self-preservation comes ahead of economy'.

While following a growing trend among politicians that strategic air power was the way forward for a national air policy, the Finletter Commission had supported the interests of the Air Force and gained the support of the general public. The Army knew it now had no role in the determination of US air power and when Symington appeared on the cover of *Time* magazine with a question 'Peace through Air Power?', the Navy could have protested an orchestrated hijacking of support. On its inner pages, it comprehensively endorsed the logic of the report and provided an answer: 'The cost of keeping alive, like the cost of living, has just gone up.'

Implementation

In a less publicised set of conclusions, the Finletter Commission explored ways in which enhanced capabilities could still be achieved within an environment of tight fiscal constraints. Noting the absence of a vibrant, post-war civil aviation market, it proposed to support a healthy aircraft industry by presenting solutions to existing problems: that an aircraft could be both a weapon of war and a carrier of commerce; a market with only the government as a major customer taking 80–90 percent of the product; violently fluctuating demand due to uncertainty of government requirements; and a lack of production continuity required to keep a trained and skilled workforce together.

It noted that there was a rapidly changing range of technologies forcing reduced operational currency, increased obsolescence and high engineering costs funding frequent, short-term changes in both systems and aircraft. With sophisticated applications of new and sometimes revolutionary design requirements, frequently uploaded to the manufacturer, the number of types and prototypes was outstripping delivery due to the proportionately long manufacturing cycles.

In these issues, the Finletter Commission identified the most important factors requiring urgent attention and posited the unheard-of notion, bordering on accusations of unacceptable government intervention that it should 'keep a few marginal manufacturers in business who might be forced out if the normal laws of supply and demand were allowed to operate'. Note that both this and a policy of allocating contracts to a diverse range of US States to satisfy Members of the House and their constituents would become practice within two decades. While consideration of diversity and the financial needs of individual manufacturers would be an important factor in deciding which aircraft to order. In this respect, in his thinking Finletter was far ahead of current practice.

Despite the powerful arguments raised by the Finletter Commission, its recommendations were never realised but it served as a landmark in the development of a national air power policy, which had been sought since the day Americans went to war in France to help defeat the Kaiser's army. In harvesting information from industry, commerce, government budget-planners, service chiefs and manufacturers across the United States, it was able to formalise an approach which defined the way Americans thought of national defence and how the Air Force shaped its doctrine for the next 15 years. For that long the bomber was central to the country's defence policy and helped steer the way conventional and nuclear weapons would be procured and what aircraft would be trialled, tested and deployed.

Truman was receptive to the Commission's arguments and agreed with its conclusions. But his stoic determination to keep America in good financial shape went right back to his State of the Union address in 1947 when he declared that 'If we are to fulfil our responsibilities to ourselves and to other peoples, we must make sure that the United States is sound economically, socially and politically'. Yet striking a somewhat contradictory tone he had also said that day that 'in a world in which strength on the part of peace-loving nations is still the greatest deterrent to aggression…we must not allow our weakness to invite attack'.

While adhering to his fiscal principles of constraint, Truman committed the country to a 70-group Air Force while apparently refusing to provide the money to make it so. In his budget presentation to Congress on 25 March 1948 Forrestal claimed that constrained funding had the approval of the service chiefs but Symington spoke up for the Air Force when he responded by claiming that the 70-group call had not been implemented in funding discussions. Congress concurred with Symington but Truman refused to change his mind, forcing the politicians to add a supplemental to the President's budget request to the annoyance of Truman and Forrestal. The bill was passed 343 to three in the House of Representatives and 74 to two in the Senate but it failed through a get-out clause allowing the President to disallow the use of that money – which he did.

In the bitterness which ensued, Forrestal took money away from the Air Force stoking resentment and a response from Symington, who claimed that:

> in making your decision as to how this ceiling should be divided between the Services you may well be deciding the future security of the United States, because you are leaving no seed corn in the United States Air Force (against the advice of both the President's Air Policy Commission and the joint Congressional Aviation Policy Board), especially with respect to its strategic striking arm.

And in a further more public avocation, Symington declared of Soviet intentions that 'when the year comes in which they are ready, if they believe they can win, they will strike…It would seem the air is where the final struggle, if it has to occur, will occur'.

If doubts exist about the direction of the Commission's conclusions it is perhaps that they were too fixated on the 'big' war rather than the littoral, brushfire conflicts and regional gains sought by individual Third World countries. In those situations the long-range, strategic bomber was of only marginal use tactically and even less value politically than the smaller fighters and fighter-bombers which would be employed in great numbers during the Vietnam War, when in the mid-1960s the bomber-bosses finally gave way to fighter-leaders in the command echelons of tactical and strategic planning at the highest levels.

The first Secretary of the Air Force, Stuart Symington was sworn in on 18 September 1947 and would remain in office until 24 April 1950. (NARA)

In a broader context, but highly relevant to this study of bomber forces, the highly visible and very public conclusions delivered to the President fuelled acrimony and vehement turf-protection among senior leaders in the Army and the Navy. With some justification, they felt that it sought to follow the expectations of Spaatz and Symington in shaping the defence budget around a strong Air Force, to serve as an agenda for relying on bombers to do the job of the Pentagon. The Army and the Navy felt that the Finletter report should have taken a more balanced view rather than serve up an Air Force wish-list for size and strength. Which is perhaps paradoxical, in that as a Presidential commission, Finletter went against Truman and Forrestal in placing fiscal prudence ahead of military might, however justified that may have been.

In response, the Navy was most vocal because it had much to gain from challenging the status quo set for the Air Force by the Finletter Commission and endorsed by Symington. In particular, by pressing its own intention of acquiring the ability to deliver nuclear strikes from carriers, the Navy was planning to request funds for a large, flush-deck carrier capable of such missions. Chief of Naval Operations Admiral Louis Denfield had replaced Chester Nimitz on 15 December 1947 and on 17 February 1948 he told the House Appropriations Committee that the carrier was needed so as to 'handle radically advanced types of aircraft required for planned operations and not capable of being operated from our present carriers'.

In defending the Navy as the nation's strategic nuclear deterrent, Denfield argued that it was better to build a class of super-carriers that could traverse great distances and strike land targets with

Chief of Naval Operations, Admiral Chester Nimitz would fight hard to obtain a super-carrier at the expense of the Air Force B-36 intercontinental bomber but would retire in late 1947 and be replaced by Louis Denfield. (US Navy)

multiple bombers launched from their decks than build numerous aircraft to fly vast distances and bomb their targets, returning over the same distance every time. The argument was countered by the Air Force, that it would require great numbers of carriers to cover the entire globe whereas the bombers operating from the United States could do that and in less time. Moreover, bombers could deploy to forward bases with no greater distance from the centre of the USSR than could a carrier task force. But the stakes were far higher than theoretical arguments over deployment strategies.

Known as the 6A, the Navy's flush-deck super-carrier, which was to be named the *United States*, was in direct competition with the Air Force's Convair B-36 and the budget would not support both. The design of the 6A had been approved by Nimitz on 2 September 1947 but its construction had been opposed by James Webb on cost grounds, accepted by him and approved by Truman only on the basis that the Navy would cancel the fourth Iowa-class battleship USS *Kentucky* and the battlecruiser USS *Hawaii*. The unification of the armed services had not been approved by the Joint Chiefs when the carrier was cleared for approval by Congress and that was requested on 26 May 1948. Opinion was divided but Congress approved funds for the 6A and on 23 July Truman authorised building to begin, when it was given the Navy designation CVA-58.

An Atomic Football

By this date the continuing controversy over service roles had reached a crisis point and Forrestal called a meeting of the Chiefs and their deputies at Key West, Florida, from 11 March 1948. For several days the issues were discussed and positions argued and by 20 March the outline of an agreed revision of the role definitions previously expressed in Executive Order 9877 had been finalised. The primary sticking point had been the use of the atomic bomb by the Navy, an issue which chafed the Air Force as it consistently tried to gain sole authority over its use. But the Air Force had its own issues with civilian control over access to the bomb and to research and production facilities.

Secretary Forrestal approved a draft of the agreement on 1 July 1948, defining the Air Force as the sole force responsible for the strategic nuclear role, granting the Navy use of the 'the bomb' with carrier-based strike aircraft but on somewhat nebulous terms. In a dinner with the Chiefs on 19 July, Forrestal tried to get clarity, the Army supporting the Air Force for its exclusive use. Symington favoured approval for the Navy to use atomic bombs if they could access targets unavailable to the Air Force. For their part, the Navy sought formal sanction to equip Lockheed P2Vs with the Mk 1 Little Boy bomb but that was of concern to the Air Force since it used more fissionable material than the Mk III carried by the Air Force.

There was more to this issue than protecting the Air Force primacy in nuclear weapons delivery, however – the shortage of bombs and the scarcity of material to make them. For two years after the bomb had been tested at Alamogordo, New Mexico on 16 July 1945, the Air Force had been worried that any strike on the Soviet Union would consume all available bombs for the next several years. Atomic bombs consisted of two primary elements, the core and the mechanical assembly. Both elements had been available for two bombs in 1945 and nine in mid-1946. In 1947 only 13 cores and 29 mechanical assemblies were held but in mid-1948 the stockpile consisted of 50 complete bomb elements and three additional mechanical assembles.

The original Mk III implosion type with an all-plutonium core ran into production problems in 1947 when production of plutonium at the Hanford, Washington, fell to a fraction of its wartime level. But production of uranium-235 at the Oak Ridge, Tennessee, facility was much higher, although that could only be used in the Mk I gun type device and this was not being stockpiled. Hence the low stockpile in 1947 as nuclear testing accelerated, this being the main reason why the Air Force was cautious about supporting availability of these weapons for the Navy.

With precise details as yet undisclosed to the Navy, the Air Force had several attack plans ready for pre-emptive strikes on the Soviet Union, primarily with atomic weapons but also with conventional bombs. Immediately after the National Security Act had been signed, on 29 August 1947 the Joint Strategic Plans Committee (JSPC) began working out how to wage such a war, to begin the following year. On 6 May 1948 Truman was briefed on an early plan known as HALFMOON but was concerned that the use of atomic bombs on such a scale might not be possible due to public misgivings. Nevertheless, research into better weapons and faster delivery processes was already underway.

Theoretical development of a more efficient use of fissile material suggested that a 'levitated' core and one consisting of composite plutonium/uranium-235 could provide greater explosive yield and a much more efficient use of the material. In three tests during April and May 1948 conducted at Eniwetak Atoll in the Pacific Ocean, the SANDSTONE series proved that to be the case, where yields of up to 49KT were achieved, more than twice that of the Mk III (Fat Man) bomb. These tests qualified a process which would increase by 63 percent the number of bombs that could be produced from a given quantity of material and raise by 75 percent the explosive yield of each bomb. This work led directly to the Mk IV, the Mod 0 of which entered the stockpile on 19 March 1949.

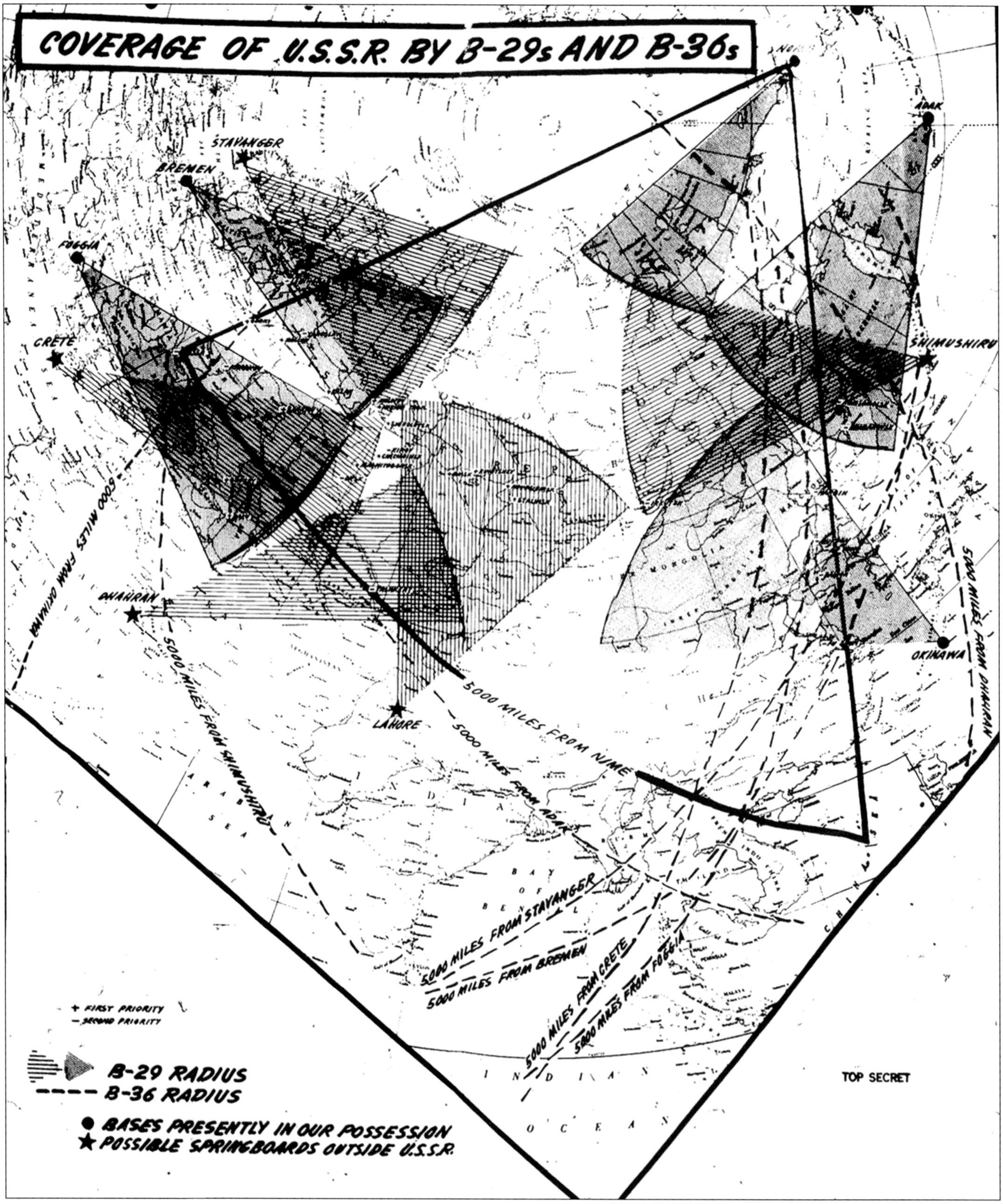

Under plans for HALFMOON, planners optimised the location of friendly airfields to assemble a series of atomic attacks on the Soviet Union using the B-29/B-50 and B-36 bombers in the event of a war with Russia. (USAF)

A model of the proposed CVA-58 *United States* super-carrier undergoing trials testing in a sea-keeping facility at Carderock, Maryland. (US Navy)

The fate of the USS *United States* super-carrier came not long after its keel was laid on 23 April 1949 but its demise had been sealed on 2 March when Truman sacked Forrestal and replaced him as Secretary of Defense with Louis A Johnson, a successful fund-raiser for the Presidential campaign the previous year. Forrestal had sided with Republican contender Thomas Dewey and his defection by switching political affiliation angered Truman. On 22 May, Forrestal jumped to his death from a 16th floor window at the National Naval Medical Center in Bethesda, Maryland, after suffering extreme fatigue and depression. After receiving contested opinion, Johnson, the fiscally conservative but loyal follower of the President's belt-tightening policy, cancelled the CVA-58 carrier on 29 April, ending the Navy's hopes of a strategic nuclear role in defence policy.

Through inter-service rivalry and contested allocation of roles and responsibilities, mission options for the Air Force and the Navy were constrained within the Key West agreement and other, modifying clauses added in subsequent meetings. The cancellation of the carrier provided a clear development path for the B-52, which would make its first flight in 1952, for the enhanced deployment role for the B-47 medium-bomber and for sustained production of the B-36, against which the Navy had pitted CVA-58.

Allocation of responsibility for nuclear weapons was still contested as the decade drew to a close but the clear distinction had been settled – that the Air Force alone, through Strategic Air Command, had control over the nuclear warfighting weapon. That football had been kicked around enough and by the end of 1949 the Navy was resolved to play a significant part, but not a prime role, in delivering unacceptable punishment on any aggressor state. The Air Force alone would have that responsibility.

An Obsession with Bombing

The struggle to establish supremacy for the independent US Air Force would be pivotal to how strategy informed procurement decisions between fighters and bombers. It would influence air power policy and shape the way the 'bomber fraternity' held sway and controlled judgements within the politically-orientated civilian leadership in the Department of Defense. As such, the underlying story of how that came about is critical to understanding how the US Air Force evolved in the 45 years of the Cold War over which it presided.

Long before the first bombing raids were to shake civilians in their homes and 15 years before the start of the First World War, in 1899 a group of international policy-shapers from several countries met at The Hague to discuss the fearsome prospect of attack from the air. Count von Zeppelin was already building his own rigid, lighter-than-air dirigibles and the prospect of dropping explosives on troop concentrations and munitions dumps was foreseen as a plausible reality. Not that it was Zeppelin's airships that brought fear and anxiety to this august gathering – there was far from any immediate probability of that – but the company had just registered its patent in the United States and that frightened many who previously had believed the country was protected by two great oceans.

The motion had been brought in a circular note from the Russians the previous year and at this First Hague Conference it was accepted, the prohibition being confirmed again at The Hague IV conference on 18 October 1907, which under Article 25 asserts that 'The attack or bombardment by whatever means, of towns, villages, dwellings or buildings which are undefended is prohibited'. It was to remain in force until the third conference which has still to take place, in effect leaving it as a ratified agreement today, one of course which is never adhered to.

The fearful prospect of unrestricted aerial bombardment was illuminated in H G Wells' classic tale, *The War in the Air*, published in 1908. In this fiction the Germans were the antagonists in an environment in which British and European aviation was about to evolve and before the first aircraft to cross the English Channel landed in England in 1909 when the French aviator Louis Bleriot put his monoplane down on a grassy strip atop the cliffs near Dover. The modern British intelligence services were formed and within five years the war which Wells foretold had erupted across continental Europe.

The origin of a strategic bombing policy began in the UK during the last year of the First World War when the Independent Force was created out of the Royal Air Force, the world's first independent air arm, on 1 April 1918. Before the formation of the RAF, pseudo-strategic bombing against German targets had been largely conducted by the Royal Naval Air Service (RNAS), while the RAF bombed tactical targets in support of ground operations. Under Gen Jan Smuts, a member of the War Cabinet from June 1917, pressure for an amalgamation of the two services resulted in the unified and independent air force but also to lobby for a strategic bombing arm, a precursor to Bomber Command formed in 1936.

The dual nature of the decision is important. Following success with the 41st Wing and later VIII Brigade under the command of Field Marshall Sir Douglas Haig carrying out attacks on Germany, the War Cabinet reached the decision to form both the RAF and the Independent Force together, integrating VIII Brigade into the RAF under Sir Hugh Trenchard and approved by the government in November 1917. Objectives for a strategic offensive included the iron and coal industries, chemical and explosives production, railway junctions and rolling stock, aircraft and aero-engine plants and airfields and aerodromes.

Aircraft equipping squadrons of the Independent Force included the De Havilland DH.4 and DH.9, roles and responsibilities being contained in *The Scientific and Methodical Attack on Vital Industries*. Added to the inventory of the nine squadrons forming the Independent Force were several Handley Page O/400 bombers. Operations began on the night of 6 June 1918 and would continue until 10 November. Strategic targets had been pinpointed during German airship and aeroplane raids on Britain since the night of 19 January 1915 but they were spasmodic and without a unified policy.

The establishment of the Independent Force of 1918, however, enshrined an air doctrine in concept if not in deed, setting up the air power balance which would prevail throughout the interwar period 1919–1939. That was initiated by the German Air Service in

The concept of a strategic bombing force originated during and immediately after the First World War and had been supported by Edgar S Gorrell (left) seen here with Herbert A Dargue. (NARA)

response to strategic attacks when it consolidated air defence units to attack the bombers, on their way in and out. Air defence units (*Kampfeinsitzerstaffel*, or *Kest*) had been set up in 1916 but with the increase in attention they were consolidated and strengthened.

Air defence was not new, Britain having woken up to a need to protect its lands from aerial attack when it was reported that a German airship had the audacity to cross the sea and fly over Sheerness without permission on 13 October 1912, and home defence squadrons, precursors to the *Kest* units, exercised the attentions of the Committee of Imperial Defence. So much so that on 27 July 1914 six new squadrons were proposed, two in Scotland, one in the area of the Humber and one each at Orfordness (beginning a long association at that location), Dover and Gosport.

By the end of the First World War and the beginning of an uneasy peace, the use of aeroplanes for strategic bombing and the implementation of home defence forces to shoot them down had been enshrined in air power policy. For the emerging cadre of US military strategists, new to the arts of air combat and bombing campaigns and without a single American-designed aircraft in the conflict, the armistice brought a time of intense reflection and re-evaluation of air warfare policy. That began with the observations and recommendations of Lieutenant Colonel Edgar S Gorrell and General Billy Mitchell.

Gorrell joined the US Army in 1912 with a view to serving in the Aviation Section after the mandatory two years in the infantry and when America entered the war he was sent to England, France and Italy as part of the Bolling Mission to gather information about the air situation and to recommend a series of options for fighting Germany. Gorrell was selected by Mitchell, who was already committed to Trenchard's strategic bombing plan, to put together recommendations about future direction and optimum use of resources. Heavily influenced by British RNAS pilot Major Lord Tiverton, Gorrell impressed upon Mitchell the great opportunity for long-range strategic bombing and that would set the tone for the next 55 years.

In the *Final Report of Chief of Air Service*, completed in 1919 and sent to General Pershing as the commander of the American Expeditionary Force (AEF), Gorrell made a strong case for an air policy based around strategic bombing campaigns in the event of any future conflict. This monumental work involved a staff of 13 with 250 people directly involved in the preparation of its final 252 volumes. The report would be scrutinised by academics, military officials and policy planners in government and among those seeking clarification of a national plan for military aviation.

The contest between the Army and the Navy was historic but experienced new levels when Mitchell contested the claim about inviolability of warships to aerial attack. To begin with, Mitchell was a proponent of air power *per-se*, but over time he quickly became an advocate of bombing as a tactical and strategic instrument for war. In his 1921 book *Our Air Force – Keystone of National Defense*, Mitchell posited that 60 percent of aviation resources should go to fighters and 20 percent to bombing operations on the basis that the former was essential for clearing the skies so that the latter could conduct strikes against military targets.

This was at some variance to the early exponent of military air power, Italy's General Giulio Douhet, whose work was published in 1921 under the title *The Command of the Air*. In it, he proffered the view that henceforth all land armies were relegated subservient to aerial forces and that war would be rendered almost redundant due to the immediate destruction of an enemy's military resources and political relevance after mass bombardment. Douhet was blind to the nuance of aerial combat, ignoring uncertainties in his assumption that strategic bombing would immediately bring a country to its knees, discounting defensive fighter forces.

Clearly, in the early 1920s there were three distinct doctrinal paths to air power strategy: Trenchard, with his view that strategic bombing had a part to play in a mixed force of warfighting machines; Mitchell, that fighter forces were a priority in any air power mix; and Douhet who strongly believed that the overwhelming use of bombing and attack on ground targets would end a war almost before it began. To endorse this, he created unrealistic estimates of the number of bombs required to bring a country down. There was simply no data available to suggest that this would be the case.

Douhet's pseudo-apocalyptic vision appealed to defence advocates and politicians seeking to achieve maximum effect for the least amount of money. His recommended use of high explosives to blow apart buildings followed by incendiaries to start fires and poison gas to deter firefighters had a macabre and sobering connotation. Especially since there was strong public aversion to the use of bombers against civilian populations, whose citizens in Germany and Britain had already tasted the effects of limited attacks from the air by airships and aeroplanes during the First World War.

Yet the prospect of massive bombing campaigns began to take root in the United States and within the military fraternity. The works of Mitchell and Douhet were set as polarising depictions of a future world in which massed aerial armadas and fleets of defensive fighters would fight over contested airspace in the skies above dense urban areas. Moreover, in evaluating the effectiveness of air bombardment, the expanding surface area of cities and growth in the urban population were highly relevant.

At this time, 60 percent of the German population lived in towns and cities, compared with close to 80 percent in the UK. The increasing density of urban conurbations resulting from the industrial revolution and the growth in empire enhanced the ability of strategic bombardment to influence the outcome of any future war. Concentrated in dense communities, an increasing percentage

Outspoken and irreverent in the face of opposition, Billy Mitchell became renowned for his pressure to build an air force of bombers to conduct strategic warfare by destroying the infrastructure of a belligerent country in the event of conflict. (NARA)

of civilians were exposed to attack from the air. Douhet saw that as a strategic vulnerability, claiming that city-dwellers were an industrial workforce and therefore a legitimate target while Mitchell took a more nuanced approach.

The debate went on after the armistice of November 1918 and in the following years Mitchell worked tirelessly and at much personal cost to his reputation, refuting the claims by the US Navy that their warships were largely impervious to aerial bombardment. Conducted after the Navy abolished its naval aviation arm, mixed results were returned from Army trials conducted between 1921 and 1923 against old, retired warships in which they did prove conclusively that they could put bombs directly on to naval targets at sea. Not long after, the Navy turned again to aviation after which it never again withdrew support.

By the early 1930s, several different all-metal monoplane bombers were competing with each other and the subsidy of trans-continental mail-carrying aircraft, together with the development of trans-Pacific flying boats sponsored the technology for fast, long-range bombers, typified by the Boeing 299 – the famous B-17. This aircraft was designed to a concept of self-defence in the belief that single-engine fighters could never be expected to escort long-range bombers all the way to their targets and back. Bristling with machine guns, the B-17 Flying Fortress was used by the Army Air Corps on very long-range flights across the uncontested skies of Central and South America to demonstrate its performance and boast its capabilities.

A Doctrinal Watershed

A decade before these events, a bomber-first philosophy became entrenched in the United States Army Air Service's (USAAS) Air Service Field Officer's School, located at Langley Field, Virginia. Renamed as the Air Service Tactical School in 1920, the courses were re-orientated toward intensive training in air tactics and in the associated techniques for junior and senior officers. Six years later it was reorganised into the Air Corps Tactical School (ACTS) when the USAAS because the Army Air Corps (USAAC), and in 1931 it moved to Maxwell Field, Alabama, the first ACTS classes opening there that September.

It was there that the doctrine of precision, targeted bombing was born, its textbooks extolling the logic in Douhet's work and in its manual on the *Employment of Combined Air Forces*. In forcefully emphasising the potential for crushing an enemy's will through extensive bombardment, it made assumptions which would never be realised, a view extolled at a time when there had been no experience of mass bombers on the scale now envisaged. Nevertheless, it was a belief that would prevail throughout the next several decades despite evidence to the contrary through the Second World War.

Mitigating its bold assertion by recognising the need for highly targeted, precision bombing of selected and strategic targets – including the centres of political and administrative power – it called for dominance of the air and the use of bombers to destroy key targets that if left intact would allow the enemy to continue the fight. It followed Douhet's belief that massed attacks could overwhelm enemy fighters, proclaiming that: 'a well-planned and well conducted bombardment attack, once launched, cannot be stopped.'

It was almost unique during the interwar years in proclaiming that by attacking key targets in an industrial enemy's heartland, it could rend asunder the very fabric of society and unravel the threads that bound its people to a central authority. It argued for a concerted,

An internationally proponent of strategic bombing, Italy's General Giulio Douhet published and lobbied for the use of air power in its most effective form with long-range bombers. (Author's archive)

Dating back to when the Wright Brothers set up a flying school, the Air Corps Tactical School at Maxwell Field became Maxwell AFB in September 1947. (NARA)

national effort involving economists, statisticians, industrialists and technical experts to define the vulnerable parameters of the bonds that bound nature-states to their endurance, revealing areas in which total air dominance could bring about the implosion of civilised society. This doctrinal philosophy would form the core of US strategic warfighting principles until the post-Vietnam era in the mid-1970s.

Concurrent with the strategic bombardment concept and the belief that bombers could have self-defensive armament to eliminate the need for escort fighters, the fighter fraternity had increasingly diminished influence. This began to have a significant impact on procurement plans and manufacturers now embraced by the scholastic influence of the ACTS orientated their attention toward satisfying the need for proficient aircraft to serve as bombers. With an emphasis on long range and the search for high speeds, industry produced some large-sized bomber contenders for procurement contracts and that led directly to a reduction in fighter requirements, leaving the Navy to develop shipboard pursuit types.

The ACTS message was exported overseas. Only a year before Hitler came to power in 1933, British Prime Minister Stanley Baldwin proclaimed that 'the bomber will always get through', a politically astute phrase which could be taken as a cynical contempt for fighter advocates or a supportive endorsement of the bomber fraternity! Either way, Britain addressed the under-performing state of extant bombers through a development programme which would attempt to redress the balance and formed RAF Bomber Command on 14 July 1936, along with Fighter Command, Coastal Command and Transport Command in the same year.

With the administrative change effective when the US Army Air Corp became the US Army Air Forces on 20 June 1941, a renewed vigour consolidated support for a strategic bombing policy to shape expansion and rearmament which was already underway in response to German aggression. While the Army set obstacles based on a belief that this prevented procurement of aircraft more suited to defensive and ground support roles, the focus on bombardment had been lobbied for exclusively within the Air Corps itself.

Between 1936 and 1939, the Army resisted any policy which threatened to move it away from the use of aircraft for defensive actions, which had been its central focus since 1919. Because of this, procurement of the B-17 was resisted by the Army and that had a telling effect on strategy. Perhaps unsurprisingly, this fight for a bomber-first policy consolidated the United States Army Air Forces (USAAF) in its inured pressure from the Army chiefs for a very different approach. A timely intervention from Colonel Harold I George of the Air War Plans Division, who until recently had been head of the Air Tactics and Strategy Department at ACTS, produced AWPD-1 which established the central place of strategic bombing in air power policy.

There had been political concerns over what was perceived to be a shortfall in air force capabilities and the difference of opinion between the Army and the Air Forces which it had overall responsibility for. As early as 1938, Secretary of War Harry H Woodring directed the then Army Air Corps (AAC) to confine procurement to light, medium and attack bombers and this was reinforced by Deputy Chief of Staff Major General Stanley D Embick when he declared that 'there would appear to be no need for a plane larger than the B-17'. Just before the Munich Crisis of 1938, the Air Corps was forbidden to purchase any more B-17s beyond the 40 already ordered.

Advocates of the bombers-first push were reassigned to secondary roles or persuaded to retire, only later being reinstated to higher responsibility or restored to acclaim when it became apparent that the forceful actions by the Army had damaged the ability of the Air Forces to fight Nazi Germany. By the time America entered the war against Germany and Japan, President Roosevelt had directly intervened to change the complacency over air power

The Italian passenger liner *Rex* was intercepted by the Air Corps in a demonstration of its vulnerability to attack. Years later, in September 1944, it was bombed and sunk by the RAF. (NARA)

which promulgated negative views over strategic bomber, all of which would create an air of bitterness within the AAF, cementing a commitment to what began as AWPD-1.

Largely avoided in most post-war historical narratives, fierce disagreement led to fateful decisions to preserve areas of responsibility and oppose interaction between force allocations. This reached a peak when the Navy vehemently opposed the Air Corps sustaining operations beyond 100 miles (160km) offshore from the coastline of the United States. It followed an incident in which AAC B-17s successfully 'intercepted' the Italian liner *Rex*, 725 miles (1,166km) east of New York, to the great annoyance of the Navy, which reminded Army chiefs that it alone held rights to controlling airspace above as well as on the waves.

These games of turf-protection annoyed the political leadership, who increasingly felt that this was compromising preparedness for conflict, which in 1939 was an increasing possibility, and on 12 January 1939 told Congress that: 'our existing (air) forces are so utterly inadequate that they must be immediately strengthened.' The story of how budget pressures got in the way of intentions has been told elsewhere but this did have a serious effect on the fighter fraternity which failed to equal the achievements of British and German designers before 1943.

Bomber procurement did improve to consolidate further orders and contract decisions as the nation geared up for wartime production, at the centre of which was the unsubstantiated belief in bombing as the strategic priority. It was in these years that the policy of US air warfighting was set while the brutal reality of real-world experiences posed serious challenges to that assumption. When the USAAF entered the war in Europe during August 1942, the senior leadership were implacable in their support for Douhet's paradigm.

Real-World Warfare

Despite warnings from the British, the Americans were convinced that problems encountered by the RAF were a product of its dislike for pinpoint bombing and a general lack of élan. General Arnold proffered the view that 'the British still have much to learn about bombing.' Moreover, General Carl Spaatz, then head of the Eighth AF, wrote to General Arnold to affirm his confidence that bombers assembled in force could fly 'into the heart of Germany without fighter protection over the whole range of operation', adding that in his experience so far, bombing operations showed that accuracy increased with enemy fire.

The official history of the performance of the AAF during the war was highly critical of these assumptions, and of the negative view of the RAF and its performance, claiming that over-optimistic assertions clouded objectivity and that these declarations had been made after limited, short-range attacks on targets in France and the Low Countries using USAAF formations heavily protected by RAF fighters. Nevertheless, when Major General Ira Eaker took over command of the Eighth AF in December 1942 he boasted that

Lieutenant General Ira C Eaker was given command of the Eighth Air Force in December 1942 and presided over a significant expansion of US bombing operations over the Third Reich and its wartime territories. (USAF)

with formations of 300 bombers on a single mission, the AAF could attack any target in Germany 'with less than 4 percent losses'.

The official history was decisive in condemning those early conclusions. And there was good reason for that. Slow to start its bombing campaign from bases in East Anglia, England, due to delayed supplies from North America and a retarded production line of heavy bombers, their performance was less than impressive. In 1943 when AAF bombers began to experience the battle-hardened skills of Luftwaffe *Jagdwaffe* pilots, losses began to increase. The mustering of B-17 formations proved incapable of providing collective security from attack and the B-17 firepower was little match for German cannon and air-to-air rockets.

In August 1943 the AAF sent 376 B-17s on two raids to German industrial targets in Schweinfurt and Regensburg in an attempt to cripple arms production but, attacked by more than 500 *Jagdwaffe* fighters, the AAF lost 60 B-17s, 16 percent of the force, with a further 95 heavily damaged, only 41 percent of the force that took off making it back relatively unscathed but with the loss of 585 aircrew, 557 of whom were either missing in action or prisoners of war. Intelligence concluded that the raid had reduced ball bearing production by 34 percent and this claim was accepted, the appalling losses justifying a second raid to finish the job.

That intelligence was shown to be false but not before a second raid involving 291 B-17s had been conducted in October where the losses were far worse, 26 percent of the attacking force being shot down or scrapped due to excessive damage with 650 aircrew (22 percent of the force) failing to return. A further 121 aircraft, 41 percent of the attacking force, suffered some level of repairable damage. But these were not lone examples. In four raids during October 1943, the AAF lost 148 aircraft, 12.6 percent of the attacking forces and around 30 percent of the fully operational inventory of B-17s and B-24s on strength and 35 percent of bomber crews.

As the AAF extended its stretch into the German heartland and deep penetration missions encountered stiffer defences on the ground and in the air, by the end of October the worsening situation brought acceptance that the AAF had got it wrong and that unescorted bombers were prone to unacceptable losses. Of great relevance to the objective analysis of institutionalised and doctrinally embedded adherence to the Douhet theory, intelligence was deeply flawed in that it logged numbers before and after the Schweinfurt and Regensburg raids presenting figures for Spaatz which failed to take account of the overall availability of ball bearing supply chains to the wider German industrial base.

This is a seminal example of observing the evidence supporting an assumption rather than absorbing the data from a wider set of parameters and reaching an objective conclusion. In this example, which will be highly relevant in post-war atomic warfighting doctrine which we will examine in the next chapter, the AAF failed completely to accept that total ball bearing supplies into Germany from Italy, Switzerland and Sweden were far in excess of German needs. Even for a greatly expanded and highly efficient war-production machine now run by Albert Speer, ball bearing inventories were outpacing the requirements and would continue to do so for the remainder of the war, petroleum and lubricants eventually being the brake on German wartime manufacturing. Yet numerous sources continue to this day to assert that Allied air raids made serious dents in ball bearing inventories, vital for almost every item of warfighting munition, at manufacturing facilities across the Nazi-run Empire.

The conclusion is, moreover, that the AAF was also selectively choosing figures which supported another doctrinal philosophy of Douhet: that strategic bombing using massed formations of attacking aircraft will suppress resistance, destroy an enemy's will to fight and bring about a national collapse. These tenets would survive into the post-war environment of a newly independent air force and bring consequences which were to the detriment of the air force as a whole.

Losses in the Schweinfurt and Regensburg raids brought a halt to US daylight bombing but with little question about the determination to conduct pinpoint raids, although that definition would be open to question. The Eighth AF could no longer afford to conduct these raids without strong escort presence, all the way out and all the way back. This would only be provided by the appearance of long-range P-51s supported by P-47s and P-38s of less generous range during 1944, when daylight bombing operations resumed. But this war would not be won in the air, although strategic bombing would be the core of air force planning.

However, lessons which were carried forward into the post-war strategic planning sessions provided some evidence that mass bombing of industrial targets worked, erosion of the industrial capacity of a nation to continue aggressive actions being most notably achieved against Japan. These results endorsed earlier claims from Spaatz and LeMay that intensive and remorseless bombing campaigns would bring about the collapse of a belligerent nation but the separate case with Germany was very different.

Lessons from the strategic war against Japan would be used to plan post-war air policy but the results of the analyses conducted

Post-war bombing plans resulted from detailed analysis of operations conducted during the Second World War, including lessons learned from raids such as that on the Schweinfurt ball bearing works which brought unacceptable losses to the Eighth Air Force. (USAF)

immediately after that conflict were used to support the penetrating bomber as the prime tool in the workbox of implements the United States would use to extend its security and construct a deterrent. Summary examination of those events show a different conclusion. Key to understanding the way air policy analysts work is to measure the effect of strategic bombing on available resources and national production levels as two separate factors.

The US warfighting policy against Japan is pivotal to qualifying the strategies and air power politics discussed in the next chapter. Analysis of the economic and strategic war against Japan is also fundamental to understanding the way policy-makers in post-war America would use one interpretation of the results to frame a bomber-first approach to procurement and operational deployment, while ignoring the bigger picture.

The War Against Japan

The Japanese economy began preparing for war in 1928 and by 1940 production had increased by 75 percent with heavy industrial output growing five-fold, 17 percent of total overall output devoted to war materiel compared with 2.6 percent in the United States. The emergence of aircraft, aluminium, machine tool, automotive and tank industries was unprecedented in modern times and would outpace the expansion of the Soviet industry under Josef Stalin.

Dependent on raw materials, resource-depleted Japan doubled coal production but fell far short of what it could domestically produce. Before war began, Japan quadrupled aluminium ingot output, 90 percent of which came from the Dutch East Indies with foreign dependence for rubber, ferro-alloys and non-ferrous metals with stockpiles reaching record levels. Nevertheless, by 1941 the potential in the Japanese economy was only 10 percent of that in the United States and a quick war was the only solution to increased resource-demand.

Analysts logging the pace of Japan's war production noted that not until late 1942 and the military defeats did the country place its economy on a war footing, resources assigned to military operations increasing from 23 percent in 1941 to 31 percent in 1942, 42 percent in 1943 and 52 percent in 1944. Despite half the balance going on food, the Japanese people were already going hungry, transport was breaking down due to loss of investment and the country had run out of ways to deploy human resources as increasing numbers of workers fell sick, were overworked in factories or died from declining health care.

Increasingly, manufacturing and services were tuned to war production, deliveries of combat aircraft increasing from 700 aircraft per month in mid-1942 to 2,572 per month two years later. Losses within the merchant fleets due to US Navy interdiction

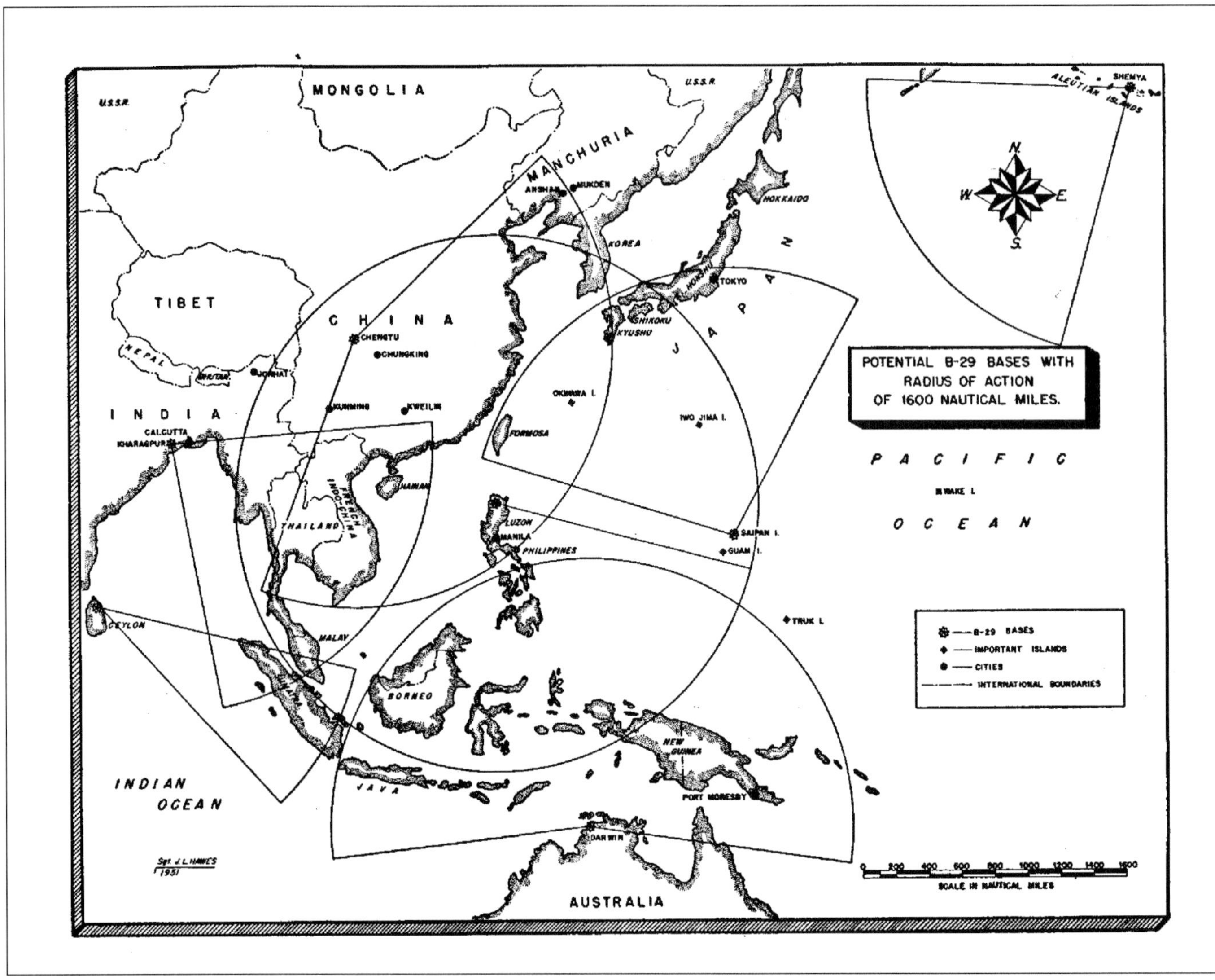

With a considerably greater radius of combat action, the B-29 was able to strike mainland Japan from a base in Saipan, as shown here with targets available from other locations. (USAF)

forced 35 percent of all steel consumed to go into ship building to replace sunken ships and maintain supplies from occupied countries down to Indonesia, with diminished allocation for warships as a consequence. By 1944 Japan was unable to protect high-priority weapons production because demand for the ships necessary to keep the country replenished reached unprecedentedly low levels of supply. Oil imports too began to decline from August 1943 and had been virtually eliminated by April 1945, levels falling so as to virtually eliminate fuel for pilot training.

The overriding conclusion in post-war analyses conducted by the US government was that without any aerial bombardment, the US Navy had virtually starved Japan out of warfighting resources and that 'interdiction of overseas imports' had pushed the country's warfighting abilities below sustainable levels 'even without direct air attack on her cities and industries'. Which was not the view taken by the Army or the AAF. Furthermore, it was the formal conclusion of the US government analysis that:

> By mid-1944 those Japanese in possession of the basic information saw with reasonable clarity the economic disaster which was inevitably descending on Japan. Furthermore, they were aware of the disastrous impact of long-range bombing on Germany and, with the loss of the Marianas, could foresee a similar attack on Japan's industries and cities.

Convinced that Japan would only be brought to its knees following a land invasion by Allied forces, it was decided to subject the country to a remorseless bombing campaign to weaken its ability to resist that assault. Similar to planning prior to D-Day on 6 June 1944, where air power was used to weaken the enemy's ability to resist the Normandy invasion, it was agreed that the AAF should be used to destroy infrastructure essential to Japan resisting attack along the Kyushu beachheads where it was believed the Allied forces would land.

But that changed when analysts fresh from a defeated Germany were consulted about the correct approach to take, proposing that, through the coordinated impact of a blockade and direct air attack, Japan could be defeated before anticipated landings. But there was uncertainty in that and studies of the type of attack needed to ensure either approach was satisfied were quite similar, with consensus supporting the destruction of physical industrial facilities followed by disruption of road, rail and other transport.

So it was decided that this would be the order of attack by air, very little consideration having been given to the actual state of Japan's societal and political state, with attacks on the rail infrastructure just beginning when war ended.

Before that, the introduction of the only aircraft capable of delivering a strategic bombing campaign against homeland Japan was the B-29, which began operations from Chengtu, China. The

B-29s of the 499th BG operating out of Isley Field, Saipan, distant facilities such as this calling for major airlift support on a regular basis. (USAF)

range of the B-29 made such raids only marginally possible, with greatly depleted bomb loads to achieve required range and only limited success. For a while it looked as though the B-29 would have minimal influence on the war effort, only 800 US tons of bombs being dropped by these aircraft between June 1944 and January 1945.

With inaccuracy adding to the ineffectiveness of the raids, each B-29 could carry no more than 4,000lb (1,814kg) of bombs across the 2,075 miles (3,340km) between Chengtu and targets in Japan. Operationally, XX Bomber Command could realise only 14 percent of its potential and the use of these aircraft as bombers gave way to B-29s being adapted to carry fuel from bases in India to China on the few operational missions authorised. There was very little military advantage in using these aircraft in this way and advisory recommendations for pinpoint bombing from high altitude could only be implemented when bases were secured closer to Japan.

This was achieved four months after the capture of the Marianas Islands, B-29 operations against Japan beginning at the end of November 1944, replacing the raids from Chengtu in a rapid transition. Now, with distances reduced to 1,400 miles (2,349km) and a saving of 1,350 miles (2,172km) on a round-trip raid, bomb loads were greatly increased and the policy previously adopted for early Eighth AF raids on Germany was implemented. But, just as there had been in those first raids after the AAF arrived in England, loss rates were unacceptably high in the Pacific too.

By 9 March 1945, only 7,180 US tons of bombs had been dropped with an average of less than 10 percent hitting their intended targets. Although bombing from 30,000ft (9,144m) and loss rates were 3.6 percent, they were effective. The Japanese leadership was worried by the erosion of production capacity and began an immediate dispersal of manufacturing plants similar to that which the Germans had undertaken. Changes were necessary to reduce aircraft losses and to increase the effectiveness of the raids.

As would be disclosed in official analyses after the war:

> Weather constituted the most serious obstacle…intervening clouds often obscured a clear view of the aiming point thereby resulting in an unsuccessful bombing approach…Bombing accuracy as a result of these conditions was not satisfactory. Urban areas, readily identifiable on the radar scope were usually designated as secondary targets since accuracy limitations of the APQ-13 radar prevented successful radar bombing of pinpoint industrial targets from high altitude.

A fundamental shift in strategy was made effective from 9 March 1945 when the four principal Japanese cities were the targets for night attacks from 7,000ft (2,133m), 1,667 US tons burning out 15 miles^2 (38.85km^2) of Tokyo that first night. Nagoya was targeted two nights later and by 19 March, 1,595 sorties had dropped 9,373

The use of fire-bombing raids against significant Japanese targets set Tokyo alight with a carpet-bombing technique which the Eighth AF had introduced in Europe from 1944. (USAF)

US tons on these two cities as well as Osaka and Kobe, destroying a total of 31 miles^2 (80.29km^2) for a loss of 22 aircraft. Accuracy increased, with 35–40 percent success within 1,000ft (304.8m) of the target point.

The switch from pinpoint targeting and attempted precision bombing to area bombing and the more brutal interpretations of Douhet – that people are industrial production units and therefore legitimate targets – instilled in LeMay and the AAF leadership that it was air power that had brought Japan to its knees. That would be endorsed in official justification for the dropping of atomic bombs on Hiroshima and Nagasaki but the rationale for conducting area bombing and its consequences was justified only if other factors were ignored. The Navy had done more than the AAF to bring Japan to the point of surrender by all but eliminating supply routes by sea and starving out critical industries.

Legacy

In post-war bombing applications and specific target planning, analysts revealed differences in data from the Second World War on each target country but the commitment to strategic bombing as the prime use of air power remained. Yet, as noted, the signs were there that this was a potentially flawed judgement. Results from the raids on Japan were controversial but the Air Forces continued to proclaim it as an unquestionable success, with people such as the future US Secretary of Defense, Robert S McNamara, serving with the Office of Statistical Control under General LeMay.

Working especially with XX Bomber Command, McNamara conducted detailed analyses of how large bomber formations could be utilised in various ways, devising operations in which the B-29s would be used to transport fuel and cargo into China from India and setting out statistical parameters for evaluating the success of the bombing raids on Japan from the Marianas Islands. Although he left the service in 1946, McNamara's work greatly influenced the approach taken by LeMay in structuring Strategic Air Command (SAC) and using McNamara's calculations up-scaled to the atomic age.

McNamara would become a rising star in the big corporate business world and had a distinguished career with the Ford Motor Company, becoming its first president outside the family in November 1960. Less than a month later he was asked by John F Kennedy to join his government immediately after he was inaugurated on 20 January 1961. The work he had done 15 years previously greatly influenced thinking in leaders such as Spaatz and LeMay but his reduction of conflict into a few mathematical equations was deeply flawed and it would take until the mid-1970s for that lesson to be learned.

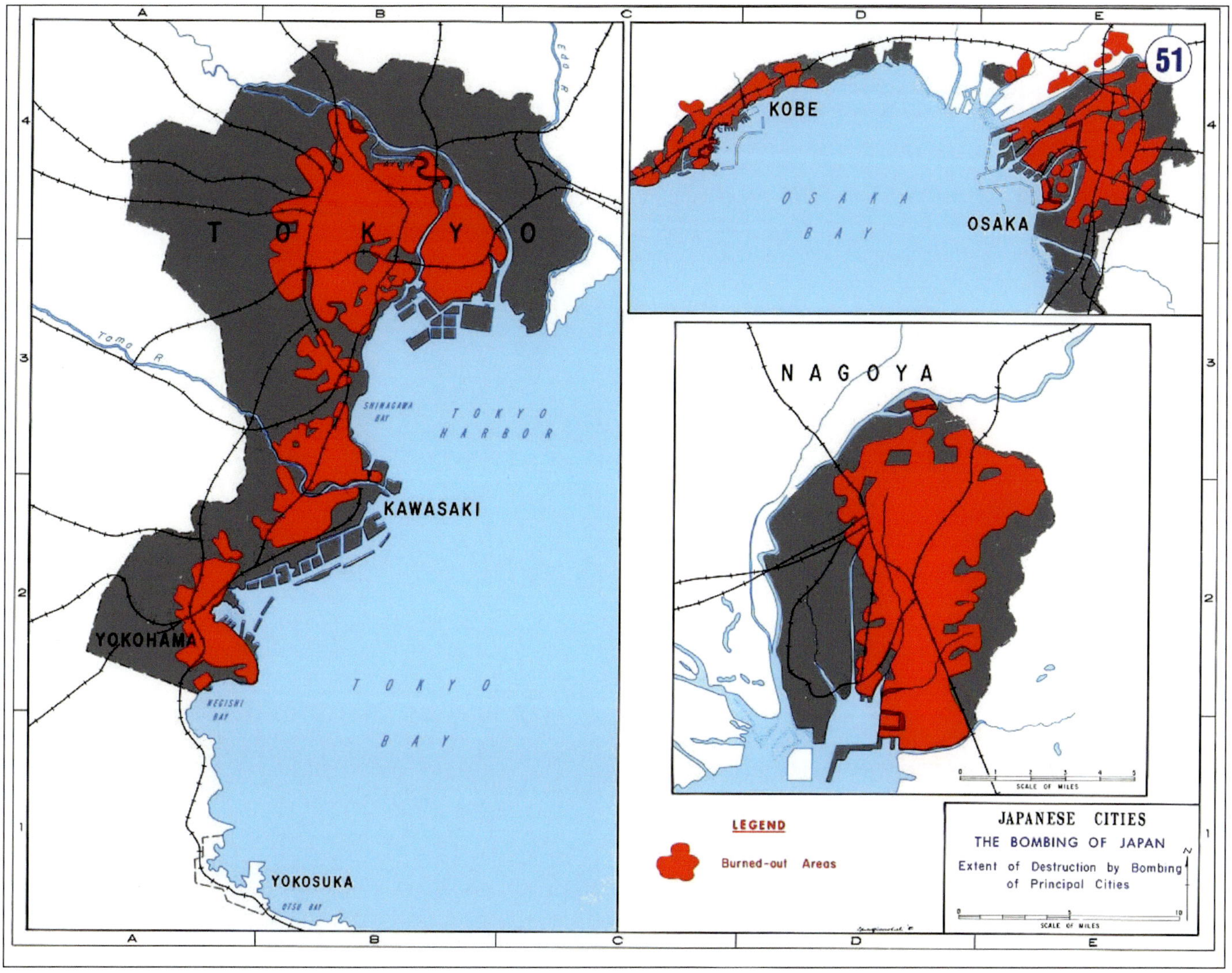

Areas of Tokyo City destroyed by US carpet-bombing raids compared with Kobe, Osaka and Nagoya. (USAF)

The analytical tools available to the AAF at the end of the Second World War should not have produced the unwavering belief in the contribution all-out aerial bombardment could make to modern warfare but there was an unwillingness to believe anything else; the door of alternate interpretations and nuanced reflection had been slammed shut. On 1 April 1945, General LeMay had written to Brigadier General Lauris Norstad claiming that: 'I am influenced by the conviction that the present stage of the development of the air war against Japan presents the AAF for the first time with the opportunity of proving the power of the strategic air arm…I feel that the destruction of Japan's ability to wage war lies within the capability of this command.'

That view was carried forward to the post-war struggle to maintain US supremacy in the air, a dangerous assertion that, fortunately, was never tested but it defined the shape and structure of the independent Air Force and the organisation which would be formed to carry that possibility to another enemy – the Soviet Union.

A balanced assessment of the bombing record does not invalidate that as a means of carrying the war to the enemy's industrial and political heartlands but the way the data was interpreted leaves question – to this day – about the conclusions that led to a bomber-first policy. Decisions of this kind affect the structure of the air force as a whole and requires associated costs and commitments far beyond the bomber force alone, essential resources including transport and overseas airfield use.

It is an incontestable fact that the AAF destroyed vast swathes of Japan's industry and that is not in question here but the destruction of physical assets is not the sole reason for elimination of a capability. Japan's capacity to wage war had disappeared before the bombing campaign began and these errors in interpretation would invoke a cost to the air force and the country itself until a more balanced and reactive force structure emerged from the mid-1970s.

Understanding this error is key to interpreting the reasons for wasted resources and a slanted balance between defence and offence which prioritised the bomber. That decision lay at the very heart of how America would plan to wage war with a new and demonstrably more powerful weapon which, had it been factored into the need for a total sea-change in policy, might have been deployed in a very different way. As it was, policy planners in the immediate post-war period harvested a slanted overview of the strategic bombing campaigns of the Second World War and voted for business as usual.

2
THE GOVERNMENT AND THE MANUFACTURERS

Four principal aircraft manufacturers provided production or experimental types covered in this volume. Each had made a notable contribution during the Second World War and all faced various challenges when peace was restored in September 1945. Remarkably, only two US manufacturers produced bombers for operational service in the period 1945–1949 and of those Boeing was the more notable, for the legacy aircraft of the Second World War and for the B-50 and the B-47. North American would produce the B-45, the first US jet bomber, and Convair would design and develop the B-36. Northrop would compete with the B-36 using their flying wing concept as an unsuccessful challenger in both piston and jet powered versions.

Production during the Second World War had been distributed according to availability of manufacturing facilities. The Boeing B-17 for example being produced at its Seattle factory, and at the Douglas Long Beach and Vega Burbank facilities. The B-24 was built by Consolidated at San Diego and Fort Worth, along with Ford at Willow Run, North American at Dallas and Douglas at Tulsa. The B-25 was built exclusively by North American at its Inglewood and Kansas City factories with the B-29 at Boeing's Seattle, Renton and Wichita factories and by Bell at Atlanta and the Martin Company at Omaha. The Consolidated B-32 came out of its San Diego and Fort Worth facilities.

There was little profit in government contracts for military aircraft and the sheer volume of production requirements meant major investment on frequently spurious prospects. The prices paid for aircraft were high but not considered excessive and the contract system in place during the Second World War was retained in large part during the early post-war years. The cost-plus-fixed-fee (CPFF) arrangement was preferable to the cost-plus-percentage-of-cost (CPPC) deal in vogue during the First World War. Industry hoped to enter the post-war years with a CPFF deal for production contracts on new aircraft when manufacturing costs could not be narrowed closer than plus or minus 30 percent, a variable likely to produce a cardiac arrest in any corporate finance office!

Both industry and government customers agreed that the 'fixed' price contract need not be that inflexible, some support being received for setting points of 'redetermination' so that the prices could be adjusted. In an industry where customer (government) changes could incur unwelcome expenses for the contractor, this was a helpful alleviation of risk. So flexible in fact that they could be regarded as variations of the cost-reimbursement method; where the government found that the higher the estimated costs the higher the potential profit to the contractor at the expense of the taxpayer, adjustment could be made.

In very short time, the government found that the wartime CPFF deals worked best for all concerned but the 1947 Armed Services Procurement Act did not always reduce complexity, conduct equitable contract deals or simplify procedures, with most negotiations conducted under 'exceptions' clauses to expedite work and move the process along. Subject to further discussion in *Volume 3: US Navy and Marine Corps Combat Aircraft 1945–1949*, naval contracts were generally written as 'incentive' deals whereby costs varying from the original estimate could be shared between

The Consolidated TB-32 production line, indicative of the mass mobilisation of wartime industrial output. (Convair)

Subcontracting and shared production became commonplace but would not be so common in post-war years. Here, technicians at Ford's Willow Run facility install engines on a B-24. (USAF)

North American B-25s in production at the Kansas City, Kansas, facility. (NARA)

A black worker installs screws in a structural assembly at the Ford Willow Run facility, skills taught to an ethnically diverse workforce predicated by the urgency of war but abandoned when peace returned. (NARA)

Wing fixtures set up at the Willow Run factory. (NARA)

contractor and customer. This form of contract would be introduced by the Air Force in 1955.

The effect on industry by the end of hostilities against the Axis forces was almost catastrophic. The Aircraft Industries Association of America summarised a dire consequence when it reported that:

> Reductions in the aircraft production program began early in 1944 and continued throughout the year and during 1945. Three separate reductions totalled 75,700 airplanes at a saving of more than 13 billion dollars. These cutbacks resulted in the separation of more than 1,000,000 employees, a reduction in the production rate from nearly 10,000 units a month to only 6,000 a month.
>
> The industry was characterised in 1945 by a constant shrinkage due to these cutbacks, to employees leaving their jobs caused by a relaxation of 'victory pressure' and a foreboding of coming cuts by management resulting in gradual realignment of facilities and a 'drawing in' of the enormously outstretched operations. Personnel continued to drop through the first half of 1945, with about 250,000 employees leaving their jobs. As a result, the industry entered August 1945 with a production rate of less than 5,000 planes a month, lowest in the preceding 33 months since November 1942.
>
> On 14 August 1945, contracts for nine billion dollars-worth of aeronautical equipment, including 31,000 military aircraft, were cancelled. This was 90 percent based on the 1946 program. The net saving was seven billions. Within the following two weeks approximately 450,000 employees were separated from the industry. Production came to a near halt, and only half-a-dozen specified types continued in production at the end of 1945 with about 150,000 employees left in the entire industry.

With the end of the Second World and the uncertainty as to where the customer base would appear most lucrative, industry chiefs examined three most likely areas for exploitation: military, commercial and general aviation. The main bomber contractors were sceptical about an early resurgence in procurement and design contracting, lukewarm regarding the airliner market and unsuited to the small aeroplane operator. As noted below, both Boeing and Convair sought some market income from the commercial market and tipped into that with new designs from invested concepts for which development costs had already been paid, aircraft such as the B-29 being adapted into the Stratocruiser. But the industry as a whole failed to anticipate the collapse of that market in 1948 until revived a year or two later.

A core concern for industry was the reduction in government procurement of combat aircraft, especially bombers. Purchasing costs go down as order numbers rise and the research and non-recurring development costs are amortised across a greater number of aircraft rolling out the factory gates. A situation in which the manufacturer can reduce the price. But if orders are cut back, unit costs go up as the same amount of development money has to be paid back across fewer aircraft and the manufacturer loses out on recurring orders. If the government cuts orders, causing an increase in unit price, it could be said that it would end up paying the same amount in total for a reduced number of aircraft because the cost of each increases.

In reality, the government can save money by paying the same amount for fewer aircraft but saving on recurring costs across the life-cycle of each one it buys and operates. Fewer aircraft cost less due to a reduction in the overall inventory but it has lost out in force-effectiveness by having fewer aircraft to do the job ideally requiring a larger number in the inventory. And the cost-benefit ratio still works there too, as fewer infrastructure items procured from private companies to keep the aircraft operating over their lifetime raises the cost of each until the net benefit becomes a negative burden on government coffers.

It was within these econometric equations that industry sought to offer cost-effective aircraft and affordable products. Several major manufacturers pressed home the economic logic of using the capital assets of industries grown rich on war profits – perfectly legal and within government oversight during the conflict – to fund sustainable procurement. They feared that a run-down in orders would starve the country of its skill-base as large numbers of workers from the aircraft industry were laid off or retired out. That would divest the nation of its lead in aeronautical engineering and set back the advantage it had over potential competitors.

Ever mindful of the dependency of their constituents on employment and jobs prospects, members of the House and Senate budget and oversight committees sought an equitable distribution of contracts and government money across the then 48 States. Recognising that American air power relied on a vibrant economy and a skilled workforce, considerable attention to the affairs of industry was seen increasingly as effective and responsive politics.

Several manufacturers provided skills training as the employee base expanded during the Second World War, fewer reserved jobs for men draining companies of their experienced work force as recruitment into the services accelerated. (NARA)

By reacting to public concerns regarding opportunities afforded to them in their everyday lives, sympathetic messages fed directly into electoral votes and were increasingly important due to the relatively brief interval between federal and state elections. At the core was affordability, of national infrastructure and national security considerations, at the centre of which was the availability of disposable expenditure.

GDP in the United States had fluctuated widely between the wars, from -12.9 percent in 1932 to +12.9 percent four years later and the pendulous spikes would be equally as wild during the Second World War, GDP increasing to 18.9 percent in 1942 before falling progressively to -11.6 percent in 1946. Thereafter, GDP levelled out, the swinging peaks and troughs would not be seen again as it stabilised at 3–5 percent by the early 1950s. The changing fortunes of America's economic structure fed directly into affordability and peacetime priorities and it formed the core of attention to how much the country could afford.

On average, from a position where it was just about breaking even, between 1941 and 1945 the United States spent twice as much as its income on fighting the Axis powers but by 1949 the Truman administration had all but eliminated the deficit. Policies and defence planning were based around the focused approach toward reducing the deficit but the manner in which the disposable components of the budget were apportioned – that amount not bound up in mandatory payments such as welfare, pensions health care and interest payments, protected by law – was a matter for government.

One element of this was the awareness that between the wars the United States had been left behind in aeronautical technology (high-performance combat aircraft, radar and engines) and that, were it to retract into an isolationist shell again, it would once more be overtaken by international competitors. Instruments had been put in place as a matter of urgency in the face of progress in foreign countries, the National Advisory Committee for Aeronautics (NACA), for instance, having been established in 1915 in response to a similar organisation predating it in Britain. But the tools provided by this national resource were used in developing commercial aviation and both national and international air transport. The resounding message among the initiated in Congress was to use the post-war economy to build a strong US air power capability and to retain leadership in aeronautics and defence initiatives.

Most of the lobbying for that was conducted with the politicians, particular Republicans opposing Truman's Democrat government which, in the period under question and apart from the elections of 1946 held a majority in the US House of Representatives until that was reversed two years later with reciprocal swaps between parties in the Senate. These factors were crucial to lobbying for air power policies and the established pre-eminence of strategic bombing

A major asset for post-war production was a workforce skilled in specialist trades sought by industries producing a new generation of aircraft, fearing to change jobs while several million ex-servicemen looked for work. (NARA)

in the Truman administration, with polarised arguments around budgets and procurement policies driven by the economic state of the country and the need to sustain investment in the manufacturing industries.

These factors are critical to judgements on air power concepts and the way the US government went about sustaining a competitive edge between major aircraft manufacturers. In both Britain and the United States, the Second World War saw a greater degree of government control and top-down intervention in the fates and fortunes of its citizens, public and private companies and related industries than at any other time in their histories. Having seized control of vast swathes of life and industry, national governments of independent and autonomous states would never relinquish that grip in democratic countries throughout the post-war world.

Market forces which had prevailed across entire industries, stimulating entrepreneurs and opening new possibilities through technological advances and increasingly sophisticated manufacturing techniques were constrained by government control and stringent regulatory infrastructure with centralised management over facilities and a government-led drive to apportion work according to political objectives. As manufacturers emerged from years of war production feeding the 'arsenal of democracy', it would now have to operate under government approval, management of opportunities and tight restrictions on business opportunities feeding possibilities controlled by the federal leadership.

Economists were appalled by what they found in the post-war US aviation industry and banks called in advisers to consult with the major manufacturers over deficits and potential defaults on loans taken out to pay for wartime government contracts when those were cancelled. By 1949 the industry had turned a corner, with Convair showing a profit, Boeing doing well with unprecedented order books and Douglas on the rise again. Fairchild delivered a 35 percent dividend to shareholders and diversification had become the order of the day, few history books today recording that Beech kept itself afloat manufacturing pie-pans and dishwashers, Cessna keeping busy pushing out tropical furniture for overseas military bases while Northrop was kept live producing artificial limbs for wounded veterans.

Manufacture of the Convair B-36 posed some challenges due to the sheer size of the aircraft and the novel manufacturing techniques applied to an aircraft which remained in development for several years after it first entered service. (Convair)

Health Cheques

The ability to sustain an air power capability was dependent on a healthy industry, financially secure and compensated for loss after cancelled contracts due to changes in expected requirements and altered circumstances. This was particularly so with the Contract Settlement Act (CSA) of 1944. As early as spring 1943, increasing cutbacks were hurting some companies engaged in production for the military and Senator James E Murray, chairman of the Senate Small Business Committee received complaints from businesses who had not received termination compensation, the refund of anticipated profits for work which was no longer needed. A War Contracts Subcommittee also chaired by Murray held extensive hearings to find out what was going on and fix it.

This activity investigated post-war obstacles to retaining a viable commercial sector for future contracts and to smooth the way for timely compensation payments. It worked its way up to the Senate Committee on Post-War Economic Policy and Planning which heard evidence from a wide range of small companies and businesses as to their fears for future financial relief when major contracts would be cancelled and compensation used to avert bankruptcy, with the certain knowledge that this would affect relatively large companies as well. The conference report asserted the principle that payments must be 'settled and paid with the greatest possible speed' so as to prevent the collapse of otherwise viable industries and to protect against ensuing unemployment. It also cautioned that the government 'must be carefully protected against waste and fraud'.

This work set up the Office of Contract Settlement which was defined as a policy-making body and not an operating agency but its director had the power to order all relevant government departments to abide by its principles. It sought to decentralise termination administration and to consult with wartime contractors and subcontractors for efficient ways to support small businesses, but not to the exclusion of larger companies where the amount of compensation could be much larger than for the smaller operators.

The Contract Settlement Act of 1944 was slanted to the advantage of the applicant, meaning that although any claim above $50,000 must be subject to review, any delay in the government reaching a decision beyond 30 days from the date of the request mandatorily awarded the company the full amount of its claim. Clearly aimed at speeding up government response to claimants and cutting out bureaucracy, it made it bindingly incumbent for the government to pay up quickly and in further respect to the needs of the applicant, it placed a time limit of 90 days on reaching a conclusion and paying compensation.

Moreover, bearing in mind the potential urgency of getting money in compensation for cancelled contracts, the claimant was to be provided with interim payments to show investors and banks that the government recognised the need and the validity of the claim and that it was, *de-facto*, putting itself up as a collateral backer to ease the sustainability of the company. There were also tax concessions to alleviate companies large and small from being penalised for non-payment of tax should it be forced to such a position of non-payment by pressure outside its own control. This model would form the basis for contractual concessions in orders placed after the war and would form the backbone of a shared investment in enterprise with aircraft manufacturers and engine builders.

A bastion of capitalist practices, the Constitution of the United States enshrined by implication a shared relationship between the State legislature and companies within its borders and between those businesses and the federal government. The US aviation industry received seed money from the government for prototype aircraft and experimental types, almost always on a competitive basis with other bidders. To demonstrate effective performance and capability, these prototypes competing for a single contract would frequently be supported by company finance in addition to the money from the government, a shared risk to do the work.

Under US contracts, unsuccessful bidders would be free to use the technology and the ideas developed under that work in other applications. The government took the view that this could keep a workforce intact and possibly create other products or programmes in related defence fields or in the commercial sector and there were many examples of that. Any such successes would have the potential to increase the workforce and turn a profit back to the government through taxes paid on that additional income.

The US government took the view that by paying contractors to build prototypes and to encourage competition it was investing in the economic welfare of the nation. But that was not the case with European companies, which struggled hard to maintain an equivalence to their American competitors. This factor is at the root cause as to why the United States surged ahead, not wholly because of a larger capital base which it certainly had, but through the way it treated its manufacturing industry in the aviation and defence sector.

In the UK, then the largest aviation sector in the democratic world outside the United States, companies unsuccessful in gaining contracts for which they had been funded by the British government were prohibited from using those products in other applications. The government viewed the funding as securing ownership with wholesale property rights and controlled the way research accruing from that money was used by the company doing the work. This prevented British aircraft manufacturers from realising their full potential, the short-sighted controls imposed by a bureaucratic civil service in the grip of overbearing government policy reducing the prospects for true independence and autonomy.

It is for this reason that development of many British-born products was exported to the United States where a more sympathetic approach allowed projects and design initiatives starved of funds in the UK finding financial support enabling further development. The importance of this difference in approach *vis-à-vis* government/industry relations allowed maximum use of American know-how to realise the potential in industry while the British aircraft industry faltered under the top-down approach taken by restrictive governments in the UK. It was also the reason why so many manufacturers in the United States were keen to compete in the knowledge that if they lost a bid they could apply that technology and design initiative elsewhere, which they frequently did to the ultimate benefit of the US economy.

Despite a sustained commitment to national defence, albeit through a shoestring budget, the US government in the four years after the Second World War presided over a transformation in industry employment. In late 1949, 250,000 people worked in the aviation manufacturing industry, approximately equivalent to those in the baking and men's clothing industries, compared with 600,000 in iron and steel production and 980,000 in the automobile industry. By the end of 1949 the economic picture of the aviation industry had begun to brighten, sales volume for airframe, engine and propeller reaching $1.7 billion compared with $1.45 billion for the preceding year.

Overall, the contribution of the aviation industry to the US national economy was small and concerted efforts were made to build a credible export business for defence equipment sought by foreign countries. This aspect of the US aviation industry had great

Table 1: Production Totals for Aircraft Types 1946–1949

Year	Personal aircraft	Civil transports	Military by weight
1946	33,254	433	13 million lb (5.9 million kg)
1947	15,515	278	11 million lb (4.9 million kg)
1948	6,969	263	25 million lb (11.3 million kg)
1949	3,400	160	28 million lb (12.7 million kg)

Table 2: Employee Count in Aviation Manufacturing Industry			
Year	**Total**	**Airframe**	**Engine**
1946	196,462	163,259	33,203
1947	179,231	145,251	33,980
1948	183,659	141,050	34,741
1949	217,404	167,441	41,180
Note: Totals for 1949 are through to June and do not reflect the total for the year. Excluded are employees in the propeller industry, which saw an increase to 7,868 in 1948 and 8,783 for 1949.			

political support and will be covered in greater detail in volumes which cover the period 1954–1960. While here we are primarily concerned with the development of air power, and in this volume with bombers in particular, the industry which supplied the tools to realise national and geopolitical objectives is an enabling part of that capability, a frequently ignored part of the story.

The drive to build large bombers had a significant impact on the aviation manufacturing industry, with a significant downturn in the number of commercial (personal and civil) transport aircraft built in the four years after the Second World War, overall output driving the steel and energy production industries more than doubling. Much of this was accounted for in the production of the B-50 medium-bomber and B-36 heavy-bomber types. The transition from fighters to bombers had begun around 1943, however, with the B-29 being largely responsible for the uptick in scale of materials demand.

The shift toward fewer and heavier aircraft changed the requirements and the order book for various metals and new steels such as the 75ST more suited to the new jet-powered aircraft of the period. That had an effect on supply chains and on the steel industry at large but the increase in overall production during the Korean War of 1950–1953 would put the United States back on a partial war-footing across the manufacturing sector. Overall, in the four years after the Second World War employment increased notably in engine production, employee numbers there increasing by 24 percent while employment in the airframe sector grew and fell across the same period in a total employee inventory increasing by 10 percent across fluctuations.

William E Boeing, founder of one of the world's most famous aircraft manufacturing names and designer of US air power front-line bombers from the late 1930s to the present. (NARA)

Boeing Airplane Company

Aircraft designed and manufactured by this company in the post-war years would dominate bomber inventories throughout the period of the Cold War. Its origin and history has been told many times in different media but here a summary review of the heritage is helpful in determining the levels of type experience with different aircraft designs. There will be a Boeing aircraft in service throughout the period covered by these volumes.

The company began when two individuals judged that the progress of aviation was so significant as to warrant their involvement in the design and manufacture of aircraft. William E Boeing and G Conrad Westervelt formalised their deal as the Pacific Aero Products Company in 1915, soon to become the Boeing Airplane Company and then the Boeing Aircraft Company before reverting to its previous name. William Boeing was a prominent figure around the Seattle, Washington, yachting community as a lumberman and landowner with wide connections. Westervelt was a serving naval officer with assignment to the local shipyard and so participated as a private individual.

Boeing's first aircraft was a floatplane, the Model 1 put together in a boathouse on the shores of Lake Union, precursor to several following types and the first landplane, the Model 4 sold to the Army in 1917 and the Model 5 floatplane for the Navy, after America entered the war. On the cessation of hostilities, Boeing turned briefly to manufacturing wood products such as bedroom furniture, canoes and high-powered sea-sleds before assembling aircraft under contract from other companies. Purpose-built designs followed with little success until the Model 50 for the Navy in 1924. The mix between seaplanes and landplanes followed before Boeing turned to fighters, at first the PW-9 of which 158 were built for the Army followed by derivative variants for the Navy.

Boeing was able to take advantage of government mail contracts in 1927 and produced a revised fighter design powered by an efficient Pratt & Whitney Wasp engine which was installed in the new FB-6 adapted for naval use and incorporated into the Model 40 for mail runs. Both landplane and seaplane designs followed, some pursuing commercial sales which were successful with the Model 226 executive transport type of 1930, a decade which saw Boeing make great progress producing fighters for both the Army and the Navy, an early success of which was the P-12 and the F4B-3/F4B-4 types.

Identified as the precursor to the B-17, the Boeing 247 passenger airliner pioneered the use of anodised aluminium, cantilevered wing construction and leading-edge, de-icing boots in addition to an autopilot. (Boeing)

Innovative in engineering and technology, Boeing married creative design with new materials which had previously not been used to any great extent for either military or commercial aircraft. During the 1930s, the Monomail sustained a shift to all-metal construction followed by the P-26 monoplane fighter which remained in frontline service between 1934 and 1938. The evolutionary line which led to the B-29/B-50 and eventually to the B-47/B-52 bombers began with the Boeing 247 which appeared in 1934 as a mail-plane and became one of the most successful aircraft in US aviation history.

It was a time of significant change for Boeing, the company splitting its interests into three distinctly different operations: Boeing Airplane Company; United Aircraft Corporation (UAC); and United Airlines. UAC would become United Technologies but United Aircraft was split off into several smaller organisations and sold. William Boeing left the company and Clairmont L Egtvedt became president in 1933. Under his influence, the company began a major reorientation to bigger aircraft and large bombers focused on Plant 2 which was built at Seattle and would see production of the B-17, B-29, B-50, B-47, B-52, and derivatives such as the Stratoliner and the Stratocruiser.

Boeing's production record during the Second World War delivered 16,149 aircraft from the onset of hostilities to 14 August 1945, consisting of 8,140 from the Seattle-Renton plants, 7,702 from the Wichita Division and 307 from its Canadian plant. The single greatest output by type was the Stearman PT-17 Kaydet of which 10,346 had been produced at the Wichita Division beginning in 1934. President of the company since 1939, Philip Johnson died in 1944 and was succeeded in 1945 by William Allen, who had been the company's legal adviser for 20 years and who accepted the position with some trepidation due to the drawdown in personnel and reduced demand.

When the war ended the company lost all orders for the B-29 and deliveries of only those in an advanced state of assembly were made. During the combatant years of war Boeing produced 16,149 aircraft but corporate-wide commitment to the B-29 and the nationwide manufacturing programme allowed little time for future projects and there were no completely new commercial aircraft on the horizon to carry it forward. For a short while, all manufacturing plants were shut down and workers returned to their pre-war lives, housewives back to the kitchens.

The end of the war came with unexpected suddenness, Boeing having been deeply involved in expanding B-29 manufacturing for what was considered an intensive period of production and delivery ahead. While many Americans had thought after D-Day on 6 June 1944 that the defeat of Nazi Germany would occur before Christmas that year, almost everyone expected the war against Japan would continue well into 1946. For that, B-29 production was ramping up to a new pace in anticipation of softening up the landing grounds for invasion. Very few, even within the armed services, fully understood the parlous state of Japan, nor were they cognizant of the peace moves already being negotiated.

In several ways Boeing was the most affected of all plane-makers, with the end of hostilities and the end of manufacturing coming with alarming swiftness. Recalling the days immediately after the cessation of hostilities in November 1918, when the company had pursued diversification, Boeing sought details of a wide range of commercial applications for its factories but there were problems

The Boeing Model 299 grew out of the 247 from which emerged the B-17, here represented by the Y1B-17. (USAF)

with that. Diversification would not come free, it would need investment and the board was concerned that it could expend effort competing with long established companies with credible reputations and well-oiled distribution networks, losing out to well-established, niche markets in specialised industries.

About 70,000 people lost their jobs while the company worked up a military transport type, the XC-97, forerunner of the double-deck, 81-passenger Stratocruiser, 20 of which were purchased by Pan American World Airways in November 1945. The Army liked the performance of this evolution from the B-29 and ordered 10 as the YC-97. Just as the Model 307 Stratoliner had emerged from the initial design of the B-17, the Model 377 Stratocruiser was believed to be a profitable legacy evolution from the B-29, alongside the C-97 and its several derivative variations for cargo and tanker roles.

Events of 1947 proved seminal for Boeing when four new types took to the air: the B-50 on 25 June; the Stratocruiser on 8 July; the XL-15 Sentinel, a non-too-successful liaison scout type renamed Scout, on 13 July; and the B-47 on 17 December. Only the XL-15 would disappoint but it was tough going in the lean years before 1948 when an increase in military business began to grow the order book. Boeing-Wichita was retooling and expanding the size of Plant 1 for B-50 and Stratocruiser work but the government-owned plant at Wichita was initially on standby status. When Seattle got orders for the C-97, production was assigned to Renton while Plant 2 was occupied with B-50s as well as Stratocruisers. Seattle, meanwhile, built the initial B-47s while production would shift to Wichita using the old Stearman facility after Boeing bought that company.

Overall, pressure on market forces from both the military and civilian customers pushed prices down and costs up, competition from Douglas and Lockheed suppressing the price of a Stratocruiser to no higher than $1.25 million, resulting in a loss of $15 million when production ended in 1950 after only 56 had been delivered. The commitment to jet propulsion gave Boeing new headaches but it brought the company out of a financial deficit and further pressure came with a prolonged strike in Seattle when the Aero Mechanics Union placed added burden on the finances. Nevertheless, a tax carryover from the Contract Settlement Act provided some relief and the company once again showed a profit.

Consolidated Aircraft Corporation

The B-36 would constitute the heavy bomber of the early Cold War years and come to dominate SAC thinking well into the 1950s. Set up in 1923 by Reuben Hollis Fleet, the Consolidated Aircraft Corporation built trainers for the Army before getting into flying boats for the Navy with his initial design, the XPY-1, a two-engine aircraft with a high-set wing supported by struts atop the fuselage and a high-set horizontal tail supporting two fin and rudder assemblies. True to its form, and to the annoyance of Fleet, the Navy took the design and opened production to bids, a contract being awarded to The Martin Company with the lowest offer.

Responding to this, Consolidated repurposed the design of the XPY-1 into the civilianised Commodore, a luxury airliner flying boat, 14 of which were bought by NYRBA (New York, Rio and Buenos Aires airline) for operations in the Caribbean and South America. The Commodore turned the company's deficit into profit and, bearing no grudge against the Navy, Fleet turned to refining and improving the XPY-1 into the XP2Y-1 Ranger of which the

A Boeing KC-97 refuels a B-47B, a provision which greatly enhanced the operational flexibility of this medium-range, all-jet bomber. (USAF)

Women workers at the Douglas Aircraft Company's Long Beach, California, facility assembling a B-17 during the Second World War. (NARA)

Navy ordered 23, the first production contract for Consolidated with deliveries beginning on 1 February 1933.

Isaac Machlin Laddon was the design genius behind the company's next flying boat, the PBY Catalina, which was designed to fill a Navy requirement for long-range patrols over the Pacific Ocean in support of US island bases and its colonial interests in the Philippines. The initial order for the PBY came in August 1935 when Consolidated moved from Buffalo, New York, to San Diego, California, 157 freight cars taking the start-up machinery for transferring production. The first flight of the Catalina was made on 21 March 1936 and more than 3,300 would be built. Seventeen are still flying today.

In 1937 Consolidated was approached by David R Davis, an aeronautical engineer seeking development funds for a new wing design which promised lower drag and increased lift incorporating increased volume for fuel tanks. Davis had designed a thick wing which at relatively moderate speeds would retain laminar flow up to 30 percent of the chord back from the leading edge, compared with the usual 20 percent of most aerofoils. Fleet and Laddon were sceptical and had the California Institute of Technology test models in their wind tunnel. Those proved negative until Davis persisted, pointing out measurement flaws which, when corrected, validated his concept.

Fleet and Laddon agreed to adopt the Davis wing for the massive Model 31 XP4Y Corregidor maritime patrol flying boat but delays in delivery of its Wright R-3359 engines, prioritised for the B-29, prevented it achieving service status. Instead the wing was adopted for the Model 32, the B-24 which made its first flight on 29 December 1939. The B-24 had been ordered in response to a reaction from Consolidated to build the B-17 under licence, which offered its own design instead. The Model 33 was ordered into production as the B-32 when Consolidated was asked to build a back-up to the potentially troublesome B-29 but only 118 were built after the B-29 proved its worth.

In March 1943, Consolidated Aircraft Company merged with Vultee Aircraft Company to become the fourth largest government wartime industrial contractor, bigger than Boeing, Douglas or

Founder of Consolidated Aircraft Company in 1923 after leaving the US Army, Reuben Hollis Fleet became active in the Institute of the Aeronautical Sciences, forerunner of today's AIAA. (Consolidated Aircraft)

Lockheed. Officially and unofficially it assumed the name Convair, a colossus among giants. Previously a division of the holding company Avco, Vultee had been independent since 1939, acquiring the assets of Lycoming and Stinson. It had produced the Vultee V-11 military aircraft which sold to Turkey, Brazil, China and Russia and built 11,538 BT-14 and BT-15 basic trainers for the Army.

Consolidated Vultee's order book was full when the war ended, with production of several military and a number of civilian types underway. During the near four years of US participation in the Second World War, Convair had delivered 57 percent of all four-engine heavy bombers, also including the B-32, B-24, PB4Y-2 Privateer, Liberator Express and RY-3 transport aircraft. It had produced more than 175,000 US tons of airframe accounting for almost 13 percent of the total national output in aircraft, producing 28,004 completed aircraft from its 13 divisions, 11 of which were manufacturing or modification facilities. In addition, it produced spares equivalent to a further 5,000 airframes.

Almost 43 percent of Convair's total output had been flying boats and amphibians, including the PBY Catalina and the PB2Y Coronado and 29 percent of all US liaison aircraft production was accounted for by the company's L-5 Sentinel, of which 3,590 had been built, and the Voyager. Peak employment had been reached in December 1943, with 101,624 men and women on the payroll, a year in which Convair delivered 16 percent by weight of total US aircraft production and 12 percent by number of airframes. Seeking innovation and labour-saving ideas, the company adopted more than 20,000 suggestions proposed by employees of more than 71,000 submissions, contributing more than $48 million in savings for the company, a workforce which bought $81 million worth of war bonds.

Convair had invested in the future production of large aircraft and in 1945 dedicated an 8,500ft (2,590m) concrete runway outside the San Diego plant at Lindbergh Field. Jointly financed by the

Designed in the late 1920s, the Consolidated Commodore was the company's early success in flying boat design, this example being one operated by Pan American Airways, but a type quickly superseded by competitors from Sikorsky, Martin and Boeing. (Bill Larkins)

Consolidated produced one of the most successful aircraft of the Second World War with production of the B-24 Liberator, as shown here toward the end of the conflict. (Convair)

company and the Navy Bureau of Aeronautics (BuAer), the $4 million runway was built to accommodate the largest landplanes then envisaged, notably the B-36. The following year, Convair opened its new $524,000 aeronautical laboratory and wind tunnel designed to test 10ft (3m) models at high subsonic speeds.

The Consolidated Vultee Corporation had a full workload when the war ended but there were immediate concerns about the future order book and a perceived need for diversification to maintain cash flow and best use of capitalisation. In retrospect that programme appears ill thought out and mismanaged as Convair tried to get into prototype houses fabricated from plastic and aluminium, experimental flying cars and through obtaining a controlling interest in ACF-Brill Motors and its subsidiary the Hall-Scott Motor Car Co.

Inevitably, cuts and cancellations followed the war and in May 1946 orders for the B-32 were cut back at Fort Worth before termination in favour of the B-36. Work on P-38s at Nashville was replaced with the manufacture of gas and electric kitchen ranges for its parent, The Aviation Company. By this time active operations had been reduced to San Diego, Vultee Field, Fort Worth, Nashville and Wayne. San Diego became the home of the Convair 240 while the Fort Worth facility was almost the sole post-war manufacturing facility retaining a wartime, government-built factory at a distance from its main plant.

Another commercial application was the Model 37, a civilianised version of a military transport derivative of the XB-36. Back in the early development stages of the B-36 programme, the AAF wanted a heavy-lift cargo freighter to support wartime operations and on 31 December 1942, it had ordered a prototype (43-52436) designated XC-99. It was not the only interested customer. News of the B-36 programme reached Pan American and it saw in the giant aircraft a potential flying boat through a derivative akin to that it had negotiated with Boeing to transform the unsuccessful XB-15 into the 314 Clipper utilised on its profitable routes from the West Coast to the Philippines.

The proposed Pan American flying boat adapted from Convair's B-36 would, said the airline, be marketed as its Super Clipper and carry 204 passengers and up to 15,000lb (6,804kg) of freight. Lavish interior décor and a staircase at each end of the spacious fuselage would serve gourmet meals to both upper and lower decks occupied by premium fee-paying passengers and facilities to equal the best hotels in the world. In February 1945 Pan American ordered 15, six-turboprop engine Super Clipper flying boats and Convair, seeing a marketing opportunity, proposed a landplane alternative.

Although a fitting prescient for the wide-body, dual-deck airliners of the future, it was too big for the passenger market of the early post-war years and an unprecedented expansion of both airfields and a surplus aircraft market bridged the gap from piston-power to the age of the commercial jet transport. Flying boats were out, the Atlantic market would control the expansion of the early peacetime years until turboprop landplanes served the regional needs of local airlines and the early Boeing and Douglas jet airliners opened up intercontinental travel at significantly lower prices.

As for the Air Force, the XC-99 cargo carrier made its first flight on 24 November 1947 and would conduct many record-breaking

A PBY-5A Catalina here flying across the Aleutians, a flying boat which operated around the globe for the US Navy, of which more than 3,300 were built between 1936 and 1945. (US Navy)

An armourer at Fairfax, Kansas, loads ammunition for a B-25 reflecting the influx of women employees during the Second World War but a group for which job prospects took a significant reversal during peacetime. (NARA)

runs between the United States and continental Europe carrying up to 60,000lb (27,216kg) of freight on distances of up to 12,000 miles (19,308km). While demonstrating to the Air Force the outstanding lift capacity and performance of this cargo carrier, it spent most of its time ferrying engines and supplies around from the United States to destinations in Japan and Southeast Asia.

While the Air Force liked it, corrosion and stress fatigue foretold its demise and it was retired out of the service in 1957 to oblivion, now resting at the Aerospace Maintenance and Regeneration Group (AMARG) facility, Tucson, Arizona, awaiting funds and willingness to restore it to a permanent display at the National Museum of the US Air Force (NMUSAF), Wright-Patterson Air Force Base (AFB).

The commercial marketplace had not served Convair well, development of the 240 costing well above estimates while a strike in 1946 lasting 101 days threatened production. Convair officials were aware that they would probably lose money for a while but $25 million in capital from war profits carried them through and the company settled down to riding out the fast-moving changes in markets and orderbooks. Initial estimates had Convair break even at 158 airframes of what were now referred to as Convair-liners but within two years that number had risen to 300 with the company writing off $14 million in costs. The previous year, in 1947 the company posted a loss of $36 million, reduced to $16.7 million through tax recovery.

The story of the B-36 programme is found extensively elsewhere in this volume but the parallel story of Convair is relevant to the company's future during development, test and production of that

A successful entrant to the passenger airline market, the Convair 440 was a development of the 240 which first flew in March 1947, a series in which more than 1,000 were delivered to airlines around the world. (SAS)

bomber, a story which began in 1941 with development contracts for competing designs awarded to Convair and Northrop. The B-36 made its first flight on 8 August 1946 and would be retired in 1949 but in that period Convair went through major changes and became involved in other programmes which would portend a very different future.

Enter Floyd B Odlum, president of the Atlas Corporation who saw in Convair's parlous financial situation an opportunity questioned by Avco, which already had 26 percent stock and was not convinced by the company's own optimistic outlook. Nevertheless, in 1947 Atlas bought 117,000 shares, giving it 7 percent of the company and negotiating an arrangement whereby Avco holdings were retired and raising Atlas holdings to 10 percent. Avco bought Convair's interests in the Nashville and ACF-Brill properties for $5 million against bank loans of $15 million.

An astute businessman, Odlum brought in Le Motte T Cohu, then president of Trans World Airlines (TWA) and the former general manager at Northrop to replace Harry Woodhead who took over management of Convair when Consolidated merged with Vultee in 1943, while I M Laddon resigned as vice-president but remained on the board. An additional flotation of 1.1 million shares of new stock, sold to the existing stockholders, brought in a further $10.3 million extra cash realising dividends in 1948 and 1949. Restoring financial stability, Convair lost $11.9 million in 1948 but managed to post profits of $3.7 million the following year.

By turning the company around, Convair directors kept the operation on an even keel as the B-36 matured toward service introduction and the airliner business improved too, the 240 and 440 Convair-liners arguably becoming the most successful short-haul aircraft into the 1960s, responsible for playing a major role in the rapid development of domestic air transport in the post-war period. The 240 took over from the Douglas DC-3 on shorter trunk routes and would lead to the Convair 440 Metropolitan of 1956 which, had it not been for the late adaptation to turboprop engines could have achieved what the Vickers Viscount was able to attract in domestic orders for US airlines.

Long before these events, as early as 1949 Odlum was beginning to sound out potential buyers, his intention always being to turn Convair around from loss into profit and sell it on for a cash gain. Lockheed's Robert E Gross looked at it and felt that Odlum's price was too high so Odlum sought interest from Curtis-Wright but nothing came of that and Atlas retained the controlling interest. But only until 1953 when the General Dynamics Corporation bought Atlas's 400,000 shares in a year in which Convair sales reached $370 million of which 83 percent was for military aircraft, making this company the eighth largest defence contractor in the United States. The company would go on to produce some of the more iconic combat aircraft of the twentieth century, a story told in subsequent volumes.

Glenn L Martin Company

Although prolific in production-line aircraft since the end of the First World War, the Glenn L Martin Company would not provide the post-war air force with any independently-designed operational bomber despite having two contenders, the XB-48 and the XB-51. Most notable during the Second World War for developing and producing the B-26 Marauder, it would fail to produce any significant new aircraft during the early Cold War years, although as discussed in *Vol 5: Bombers 1950–1953*, it played a seminal role in developing the impressive British Canberra into the outstanding B-57 for the Air Force.

In service with the Army Air Corps from 1934 and seen here during exercises over Oahu, Hawaii, the Martin B-10 had a top speed greater than that of any US pursuit aircraft in service at that time, revolutionising the push for monoplane fighters with closed cockpits and retractable landing gear. (NARA)

The company was founded in August 1912 by Glenn Luther Martin to build training aircraft before merging with the Wright Company to form the Wright-Martin Aircraft Company. That did not go as expected and Martin formed a second Glenn L Martin Company in 1917 with headquarters in Cleveland, Ohio. After producing several types for low-run production, Martin received an order for its first large bomber, the MB-1, in January 1918, but as the government owned the manufacturing rights it placed production orders for 110 with Curtis, LWF Engineering and Aeromarine instead.

During the interwar years, Martin would produce the B-10 in service from 1934 as the first all-metal, monoplane bomber for the USAAC and a technological wonder of its time. Considerably faster than any of the existing biplane bombers and capable of outpacing contemporary fighters, it changed the design approach for all bombers thereafter. This significantly influenced new and emerging proposals and was a major factor in giving the United States the kind of aircraft it would seek in the closing years before the country entered the Second World War. In total, 348 B-10 bombers were built and delivered.

Equally impressive, three Martin M-130 Clipper flying boats were built in 1935 following a requirement set by Pan American World Airways to cover Pacific Ocean routes and support a potentially lucrative market for commercial operations. Weekly flights were scheduled from San Francisco, California, to Manila in the Philippines with stops at Honolulu, Midway Island, Wake Island and Guam. All three were lost to accidents, in 1938, 1943 and 1945.

But experience with the design and development of flying boats would contribute toward the success of Martin's PBM Mariner which made its first flight in February 1939 with production of 1,366 by 1949. The final Martin flying boat, the JRM Mars was flown in 1942 as a long-range transport aircraft while a still larger design, the Martin 193 lost out to the Hughes H-4 Hercules.

Concerns about prospects in the post-war period received major attention from the senior leadership in 1944, a concentrated study being made of industries which the company believed it could enter, including aircraft parts and new plastics emerging from the manufacturing industry. Martin built a factory for production of polyvinyl chloride which was sought for production of flexible fuel tanks. But these were supplementary businesses and the company refocused attention on the commercial market by developing its 2-0-2 as an intended successor to the DC-3 but the type was withdrawn after structural wing deficiencies were revealed which led to the 4-0-4 with a pressurised cabin of which 103 were built.

The detailed research conducted by Martin aimed its future at the short-haul market of 400 miles (644km) on the basis that twin-engine aircraft then had an operating cost of 40–45 cents/mile compared to 70–85 cents/mile for four-engine types. Utilising some of the 3,000 P&W R-2800 engines redundant to use by the military, Martin used these for its small airliners and showed that break-even would occur on sales of 360–400, confidence boosted by predictions of orders hovering around 500. They never made it and the 4-0-4 lost out to Convair's 240. Competition kept prices down while development costs persistently exceeded predictions.

Like several other contractors of its day, Martin received assistance in debt financing from the Reconstruction Financing Corporation (RFC), an organisation set up after the 1929 stock market crash as a way of insulating the 24,000 independent US banks from collapse and extended to embrace industry and manufacturing. During the Second World War it helped provide backing for expansion into production for essential materiel and to provide interim financing to avoid bankruptcy. It survived far beyond the original intention but it would decline in purpose and be wound up in 1957.

Losing out to the B-47, the XB-48 had been cancelled in 1948. Using the RFC, the following year Martin received $44 million to

Martin made a name for itself with a range of flying boats, as with this PBM-3E Mariner spotted during a take-off run in 1942. (US Navy)

keep itself afloat as the company had no substantive military orders to offset a worsening financial crisis over its commercial plans. As noted earlier, in 1951 it would again lose out to the Canberra, the company kept afloat by receiving the contract to adapt that aircraft into the highly successful B-57. Martin would clear its debts in 1953 and the B-57 continued in production with the last of 403 delivered in 1957 as the company diversified into rockets, missiles and nuclear reactors, merging with American-Marietta Corporation in 1961 and then with the Lockheed Corporation to become Lockheed Martin in 1995.

North American Aviation

It began in December 1928 as a holding company with a tight range of related interests in aviation, ancillary supplies and airlines but the Air Mail Act in 1934 which prohibited vested interest under one umbrella forced a breakup and it became a manufacturing company while holding its interest in Eastern Air Lines. In 1934 James H 'Dutch' Kindelberger left Douglas and joined North American as the president and general manager, while J L 'Lee' Atwood, his fellow colleague at Douglas also joined NAA to become its chief engineer, soon to become vice-president and deputy general manager.

These two men would shape North American Aviation into one of the most successful and diverse aircraft, and eventually aerospace design and manufacturing operations in the United States. A year before they joined NAA, General Motors took a controlling interest in the company and Kindelberger organised the movement of the operation from Dundalk, Maryland, to Los Angeles, California where the flying weather was better for concentrating on army support and training aircraft beginning with the NA-16, the first of more than 17,000 trainers the company would eventually build.

As noted in *Volume 1: Fighters 1945–1949*, North American moved into combat aircraft design during the second half of the 1930s with the B-25 Mitchell medium bomber, the aircraft by which the 'Doolittle Raiders' took the war to Tokyo from the deck of the USS *Hornet* in April 1942. Contemporaneously, NAA would also produce the P-51 Mustang, developed into the most successful escort fighter of its time. NAA also proposed a new medium bomber capable of high-altitude flight, produced for the AAC as the XB-28, developed from the design of the B-25 but with striking resemblance to the Martin B-26 Marauder. Rejected as a bomber, the AAC ordered a second aircraft, the XB-28A as a prototype photo-reconnaissance type but it crashed off the coast of California in 1943.

During the immediate post-war years, NAA sought business in related fields such as missiles, rockets, propulsion and high-speed research while producing an aircraft which would narrowly seize the honour of the being the first aircraft to go supersonic – the F-86 Sabre, covered in *Volume 1: Fighters 1945–1950* and in subsequent chronological periods in later volumes of this series. It also sought work in the field of atomic energy research and in supersonic wind tunnels. While developing the B-45, NAA invested in the Navy AJ-1 attack bomber (see *Volume 3: US Navy and Marine Corps Combat Planes*) and in the North American Test Instrumentation Vehicle (NATIV) research missile powered by a rocket motor and fired from a 125ft (38m) tall launch tower with radar and telemetering devices relaying 32 types of information to the ground.

With peace came major decisions about the future direction of North American but the aversion to get into the commercial sector would later bring regrets as the company increasingly secured contracts for military work. Employment had fallen as low as 5,000 in 1946 but that quickly picked back up due to the military aircraft in development and production. The XP-82 Twin Mustang had flown on 16 June 1945 and would be retained as a radar-equipped night fighter used effectively during the Korean War. Unfortunately for North American, the B-45 would not attract the attention hoped for, the Air Force never being very enthusiastic in the post-war period for aircraft it believed were more suited to the army support role which it disliked, although it considered it good for the reconnaissance role.

To accommodate workspace, NAA acquired the old Vultee-Downey plant as the company pressed on with the Navy's AJ-1 Savage but that too failed to make it as the nuclear bomber intended, serving instead as a tanker. In corporate moves, North American became independent of General Motors on 3 June 1948 when that company sold its holding to the public, disappointed not to have

Made famous by its exploits when General Doolittle took it on a raid against Tokyo in April 1942, the North American B-25 Mitchell went on to make a credible name for itself in every theatre of operations during the Second World War. (USAAF)

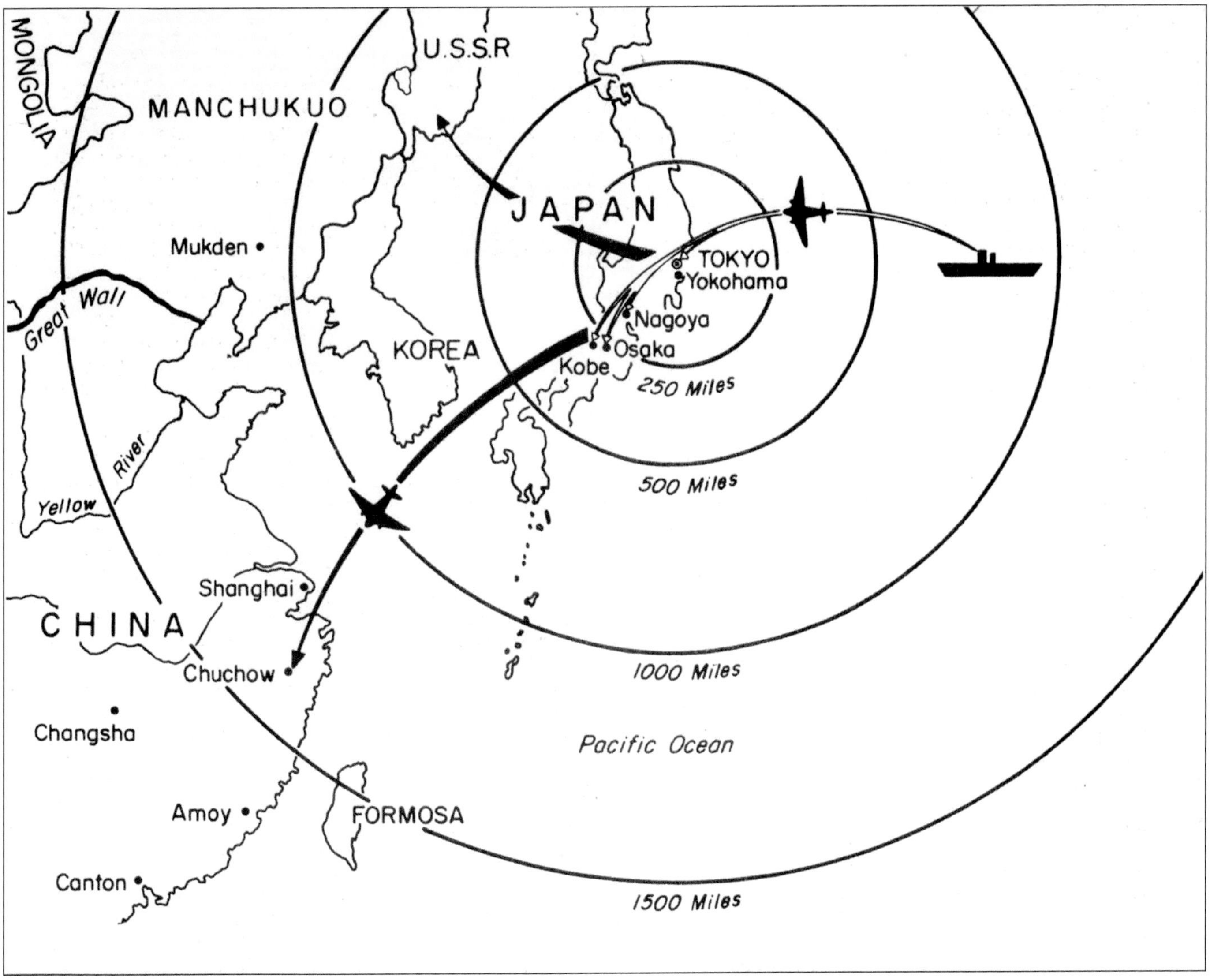

The initial strike against Japan was conducted by B-25 Mitchell bombers launched from the USS *Hornet* in April 1942 in what is forever remembered as the Doolittle Raid. (USAF)

More a development tool for introducing jet aircraft types to bomber units, the B-45 was a credible aircraft for its time but had greater success as a reconnaissance platform, in which role it provided important information. (USAF)

the commercial market it had hoped for and unable to use any of its services or knowledge for the military aircraft market. At this point Kindelberger became chairman of the board as well as chief executive and Atwood became president. This team would carry North American through the next decade, although both would worry over the lack of diversity, which would eventually come back to bite the company, as we will examine in future volumes.

Immediately after the war, North American invested in its biggest research and development programme beginning with construction of a new high-altitude pressure chamber for creating a diverse range of climates with test facilities for new aircraft and for evaluating new concepts. In 1949 it completed the second of two supersonic wind tunnels, the largest in the country at that time and built in Los Angeles over a three-year period. It had a 16in x 16in (40.6cm x 40.6cm) chamber for testing sections up to Mach 5. This paired with the 38ft (11.5m) vacuum chamber highly visible to arrivals and departures at Los Angeles International Airport and associated facilities included a dry air storage chamber and air drying equipment together with pump and control buildings.

During March 1949, the Atomic Energy Commission (AEC) awarded a contract to North American for research into nuclear reactor technology and this was to be coordinated with the AEC's National Laboratories network across the country. The company wanted to engage with nuclear reactor design and studied a low-power unit which it believed would be beneficial to other companies working in this field. In that way, NAA hoped it could secure a central role for nuclear research in medicine, biology, agriculture and industrial processes. Added to this was a new venture for testing small rockets and guided missiles in high-altitude and high-temperature environments, including air-to-air weapons for fighters and attack aircraft.

By 1949 the company reported an estimated net income of $5.195 million after taxes for the period from 1 October 1948 to 30 June 1949 with total sales and other income reaching $93.3 million. The costs of sales and other expenses were $84.735 million with provision of $3.370 million in federal income taxes. Unfulfilled orders at 30 June were $238.012 million and two dividends of 50 cents each per share were awarded on the company's 3.435 million capital stock base. Financiers were confident the company had a potentially bright future and that expectation would fund additional defence and non-defence related projects and acquisitions as will be seen in future volumes.

Northrop Corporation

During the first half of the twentieth century, aircraft companies were invariably a product of one man's dream or a shared vision with a colleague or associates. Born in New Jersey in 1895, Jack Northrop spent his early years in Santa Barbara, California, and at the age of 21 he joined the Loughead Aircraft Manufacturing Company. When America entered the war in 1917, Jack joined up and served in the Army Signal Corp but after six months he was returned to his original job, which was a reserved occupation.

In 1923 he joined Douglas Aircraft Company and gained experience with aeronautical engineering as part of the team for the Round-the-World-Cruiser, a group of converted DT Army torpedo-bombers authorised to attempt a flight around the world. Northrop left four years later and returned to Loughead just after it had become the Lockheed Aircraft Company. There, Jack Northrop

In 1945, the US Army Air Forces operated a huge fleet of Boeing B-17 bombers, the most advanced version of which was the B-17G. In service since 1942, this was built in huge numbers (4,035 by Boeing in Seattle, 2,250 by Vega, and 2,395 by Douglas). Improved turbos increased power at high-altitude, however, it was weighed down by armament (including the chin-mounted turret) and other equipment that caused drag and lowered its operational speed. Although it eventually helped to defeat the Luftwaffe, by 1945 the B-17G was obsolete due to the appearance of rocket and jet-powered German fighters, and a host of other weapons. (Artwork by Jean-Marie Guillou)

At the conclusion of the Second World War, the US armed forces were rapidly demobilised on a large scale. In need of a long-range search and rescue aircraft, the United States Coast Guard acquired 18 factory-new B-17Gs from surplus stocks of the USAAF. Suitably adapted, these entered service under the designation PB-1G. The US Army Air Forces then followed in fashion, developing a variant that carried a lifeboat slung underneath the fuselage, which could be dropped to survivors in the water with use of a parachute. A total of 130 were acquired, of which 12 received the new designation B-17H, while five operated for training purposes were designated TB-17H. In 1948, both variants were redesignated SB-17G. (Artwork by Jean-Marie Guillou)

As aviation technology was making dramatic leaps forward, thousands of hopelessly outdated B-17s were mothballed after 1945: those still in service were rebuilt into passenger airliners, or served in transport, photoreconnaissance, and patrol roles, while others were used as remotely controlled drones, or for experimenting with new engine designs (including those for the future B-52) and weapons. One rather unusual use for B-17s was related to testing of US-made copies of the German-designed V-1 'Buzz Bomb'. Manufactured by Republic-Ford, these were designated as JB-2 by the USAAF (and LTV N-2 by the US Navy), and originally planned for use during the invasion of Japan. After the war, JB-2s played a significant role in the development of tactical surface-to-surface missiles. (Artwork by Jean-Marie Guillou)

The Consolidated-Vultee B-24 Liberator was the second most famous heavy bomber type in service with the USAAF during the Second World War. By 1945, the principal sub-variants in service were the B-24G, H, and J, of which 10,208 were built by Convair, North American, Ford, and Douglas. Despite their equipment with turbocharged engines in oval cowls, more fuel and armament, and many other detail changes, they proved more vulnerable to combat damage than the B-17. Under Project Aphrodite, war-weary examples were often rigged with explosives, TV and radio guidance and deployed as guided bombs against hardened targets in Northern Europe. (Artwork by Jean-Marie Guillou)

Realising the obsolescence of the B-24's design, in 1944 Consolidated quickly developed an entire family of transport versions. They became known as C-87 Liberator Express to the Army (illustrated here is one of the sub-variants), RY-3 to the Navy, and C.VII and C.IX to the RAF. Initially used as fast transports to haul spares and supplies to forward USAAF bases, they saw intensive deployment in supporting the evacuation of POWs following the capitulations of Nazi Germany and Japan, and subsequently served for several years longer. (Artwork by Jean-Marie Guillou)

The Royal Air Force of Great Britain was a prolific customer for B-24s, and acquired them for Coastal Command (primarily for anti-submarine operations, where they played a crucial role in the Battle of the Atlantic), Bomber Command, and for the British Overseas Airways Corporation (BOAC). During the Second World War, Liberator IIs were reconfigured to serve as unarmed long-range cargo carriers, primarily for traffic to Egypt (via Spain), and then in the evacuation of Java in the East Indies. BOAC also deployed them on trans-Atlantic services and other long-range routes. (Artwork by Jean-Marie Guillou)

The Boeing B-29 Superfortress was the most advanced weapons system developed during the Second World War, and their development and series production was one of the biggest tasks in the history of aviation. Based on a requirement for a bomber with pressurised cabin and tricycle landing gear from 1938, the type set entirely new standards in terms of armament, airborne systems, and even basic structure. Deliveries began in 1943, and the crews initially struggled with the new and challenging B-29, which suffered very serious engine-related problems. However, all the issues were gradually solved and by 1945, 20 groups forward deployed in the Marianas regularly sent 500 B-29s to flatten and burn dozens of Japanese cities. (Artwork by Jean-Marie Guillou)

Despite significant engine-related problems, the B-29 gradually matured into a highly effective bomber. Unsurprisingly, it was the logical choice for the first carrier of the US-made nuclear weapons. For this purpose, the Glenn L Martin Company (nowadays part of Lockheed-Martin) was contracted with production of 65 examples to the SILVERPLATE specification. This included an extensively modified bomb bay (with pneumatic doors and British bomb attachment and release systems), reversible pitch propellers (with more braking power on landing), and improved engines (with fuel injection and better cooling). In turn, all the protective armour and gun turrets were removed. Amongst the aircraft in question was the B-29-45-MO serial number 44-86292, personally selected by Colonel Paul W Tibbets Jr. of the 509th Composite Group and named *Enola Gay*. On 6 August 1945 it became the aircraft to drop the first nuclear weapon in the attack on Hiroshima. (Artwork by Jean-Marie Guillou)

Like *Enola Gay*, the B-29 that dropped the second nuclear bomb in anger was a B-29 built by Martin and adapted to the SILVERPLATE standard. The aircraft in question was B-29-36-MO, named *Bockscar* (sometimes referred to as 'Bock's Car') after captain Frederick C. Bock, and assigned to the 393rd Bombardment Squadron, 509th Composite Group. After its transfer to Tinian, *Bockscar* flew 13 training and practice missions over Japan, before, on 9 August 1945, dropping the second nuclear bomb on the city of Nagasaki, while piloted by Major Charles W. Sweeney. While *Enola Gay* is on display at the National Air and Space Museum, Steven F. Udvar-Hazy Center, in Washington D.C., *Bockscar* is on permanent display at the National Museum of the USAF, at Dayton, in Ohio. (Artwork by Jean-Marie Guillou)

As with the B-17Bs, after the end of the Second World War, dozens of B-29s were reconfigured to the SB-29 Super Dumbo configuration for the search and rescue role and carried a droppable EDO A-3 lifeboat under the fuselage. Notably, they retained all of their armament except for the forward lower turret which was replaced with a radar. Other equipment included additional radios, provisions and survival kits, smoke markers, and extra crewmembers. The first SB-29s were received by the Air Rescue Service in February 1947 and saw intensive service for about a dozen years, especially in support of USAF units flying long-range missions over water. (Artwork by Tom Cooper)

From 1945, dozens of B-29s were repurposed to serve as testbeds for a range of very different purposes. One of the most prolific resulting variants was the EB-29, deployed as 'mothership' for numerous research projects, for example to air-launch Bell X-1 supersonic research rocket aircraft, for Cherokee rockets, or for testing ejection seats. This example was converted to carry and test the XF-85 Goblin 'parasite fighter' (detailed in Volume 1) designed for installation on the Convair B-36 bomber on long-range operations over the USSR. Another, similar variant was the XB-29G, modified to carry prototype jet engines in their bomb bays, which were lowered into the air stream to conduct tests and take measurements. (Artwork by Tom Cooper)

Based on a requirement for an effective aerial tanker, the KB-29M came into being in 1946–1947. Initial examples were equipped with the British-developed grappling system with which the tanker would unreel its hose towards the receiving aircraft, which would the grab it and reel it in via a complex and time-consuming process. This was the system used by this KB-29M to refuel the B-50A *Lucky Lady II* during her famous circumnavigation of the globe in 1949. KB-29Ms served with the 43rd and 509th Air Refuelling Squadrons (at Davis-Monthan and Walker AFBs, respectively), primarily providing training for strategic bombardment and in-flight refuelling operations to meet the rapidly growing commitments of the Strategic Air Command, from 1951 to 1953. (Artwork by Tom Cooper)

A major sub-variant of the B-29 that emerged during the final stages of the Second World War was the F-13/F-13A: a total of 118 B-29BWs and B-29As were converted to this photoreconnaissance version which included three K-17B, two K-22, and one K-18 cameras. In 1945, F-13/F-13As were redesignated as FB-29Js, and in 1948 to RB-29 and RB-29A. In February 1949, the 91st Strategic Reconnaissance Wing received its first RB-29s and then forward deployed to Yokota, in Japan, in December 1950. Attached to the 15th Air Force, the unit flew reconnaissance operations over the Korean Peninsula and close to Soviet airspace, where several of its aircraft were shot down. RB-29A 42-9400 *Tiger Lil* was felled by Soviet MiG-15s on 7 November 1954. (Artwork by Tom Cooper)

Another highly important variant of the B-29 to emerge in the late 1940s was the weather-monitoring WB-29A. While mostly deployed on standard data-collecting operations, this version was also used to fly into the eye of hurricanes or typhoons, and for sampling radioactive materials after nuclear tests. For example, on 3 September 1949, it was a WB-29 underway from Japan to Alaska that recovered radioactive debris from the first Soviet atomic bomb test, undertaken on 29 August. (Artwork by Tom Cooper)

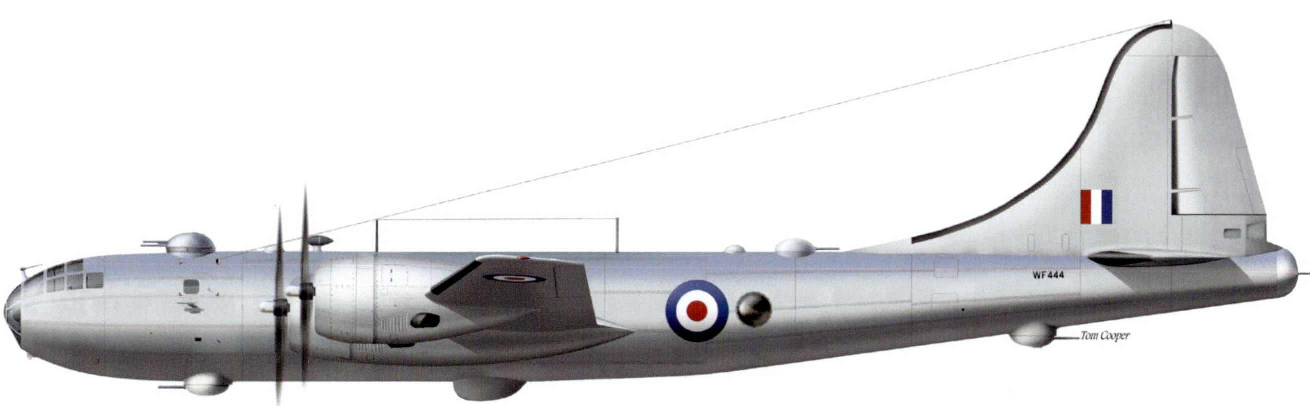

The B-29 became the only bomber of US origin with strategic reach to ever be exported. Searching for a platform big enough to carry contemporary nuclear bombs, in March 1950 the Royal Air Force acquired 87 B-29s for its Bomber Command. Sourced from the USAF's reserve, the aircraft were taken out of mothballs, overhauled, and re-engined with fuel-injected Wright R-3350-57M engines. Deliveries of the resulting Washington B.Mk 1s to the 35th Washington Conversion Squadron began later the same year. This example was a former B-29A serial 42-94502, which in RAF service carried the serial WF444. Three RAF Washingtons were modified for electronic intelligence gathering purposes and they served with No. 192 Squadron until 1958. (Artwork by Tom Cooper)

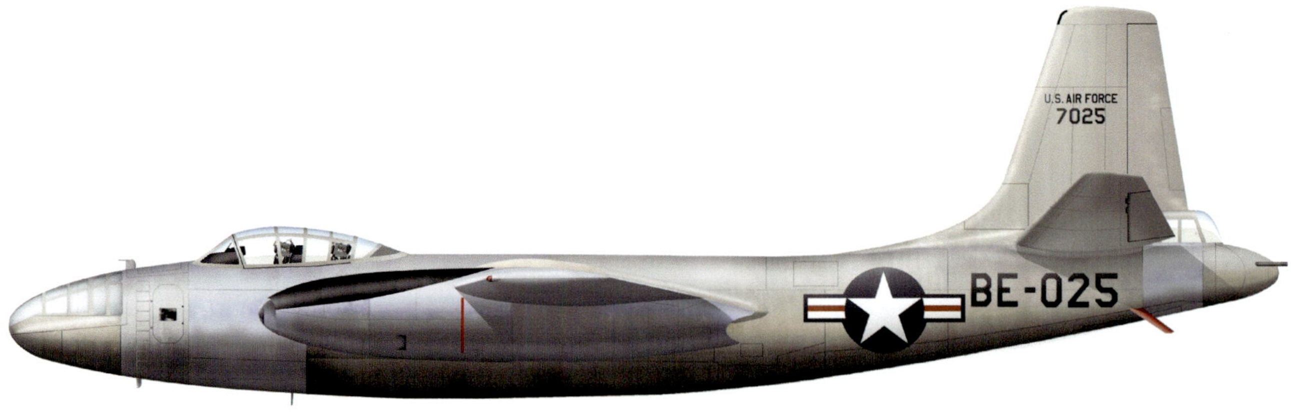

The first jet-powered bomber to enter service with the US Air Force was the North American B-45 Tornado. Developed in a great hurry in late 1944, it was designed before German data on swept wings became available. The B-45 was first flown in 1947 and entered service in 1948 to bridge the gap until the more advanced Boeing XB-47 and Martin XB-48 could be completed. Series production numbers were repeatedly reduced: only 96 B-45As were manufactured in 1948–1949, while the B-45B – equipped with a radar fire control system – was completely cancelled. Most B-45As were eventually upgraded to the B-45C standard, which included the installation of large, 4,252-litre wing-tip fuel tanks. (Artwork by Tom Cooper)

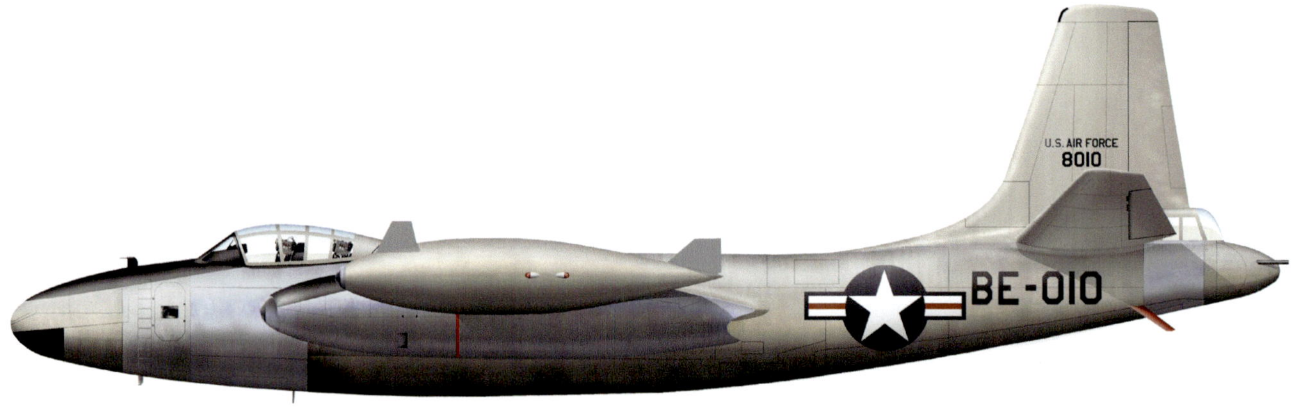

The B-45C was a heavier variant with a strengthened airframe, single-point refuelling system, and water injection systems for more powerful General Electric J47-15 engines. However, with the design already considered to be obsolete, only 43 were ever ordered, and just 10 manufactured. Nevertheless, they served as examples for a major upgrade of surviving B-45As. Early operations of both variants were plagued by engine-related problems, which undermined the type's reputation: this was to change only once the USA entered the Korean War in 1950. Starting in that year, under Operation Fandango, surviving B-45Cs were modified for deployment of nuclear bombs. (Artwork by Tom Cooper)

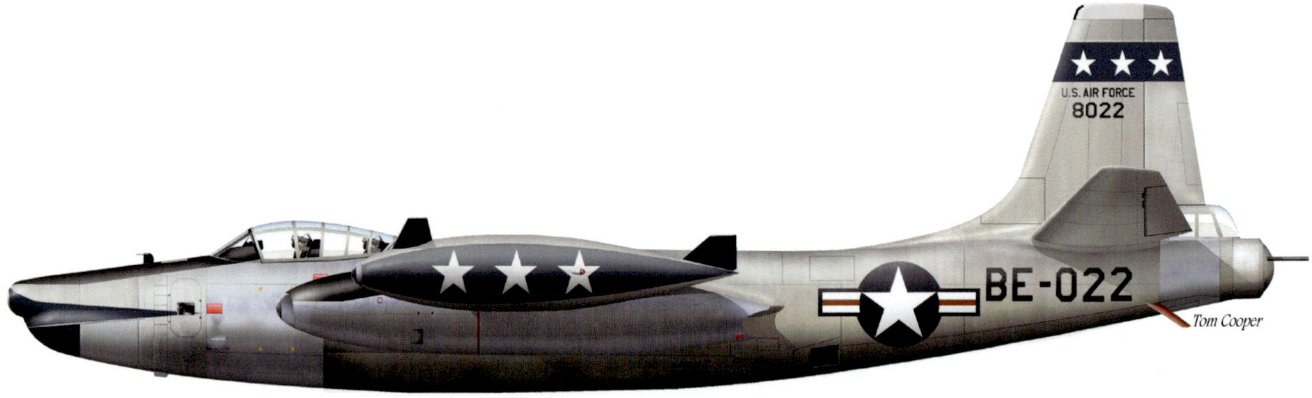

Perhaps the most famous variant became the RB-45C: a dedicated reconnaissance aircraft, 33 of which were acquired by the USAF. All were assigned to the 91st Strategic Reconnaissance Wing and heavily utilised for operations over the Soviet Union. RB-45Cs were equipped for in-flight refuelling and on 29 July 1952 one made the first non-stop trans-Pacific flight with support of two KB-29s. This example is shown as after being phased out from the 91st SRW, and assigned to the 19th Tactical Reconnaissance Squadron, which saw frequent forward deployments to Europe in the mid-1950s. Meanwhile, in 1951–1952, as part of operation Ju-jitsu, four RB-45Cs were handed over to an RAF unit, composed of crews from Nos. 35 and 115 Squadrons, for overflights of the USSR.

When Japan capitulated on 2 September 1945 a staggering 5,092 B-29 bombers were cancelled with the stroke of a pen. These included 200 B-29Ds: an entirely new version with extremely powerful Pratt & Whitney R-4360 Wasp Major radial engines, a much lighter airframe and wing made of significantly stronger alloys, a taller fin, and hydraulically boosted rudder. To save this project, in December 1945 it was re-designated the B-50, and an order for 60 was placed. The resulting B-50A become the final piston-engined bomber of the US Air Force but also served as its backbone in the late 1940s and the early 1950s, by when it was equipped with an in-flight refuelling system. Between 26 February and 2 March 1949, the B-50A serial number 46-010, named *Lucky Lady II*, circumnavigated the globe in a non-stop flight, the first such successful undertaking by a fixed-wing aircraft. (Artwork by Tom Cooper)

Following 79 B-50As and 45 B-50Bs, the improved B-50C/B-54 variant was cancelled, but 222 B-50Ds were ordered to fill the gap until jet-powered bombers like the B-36 and B-47 became available. Through 1948–1950, the 2nd, 43rd, 93rd, 97th, 306th, and 509th bombardment wings were re-equipped with B-50s, whilst 301st Bombardment Wing received a few B-50As for non-operational training only. The primary task was delivery of nuclear bombs. This B-50D (serial number 47-101) was named *Thunder Bird* and served with the 43rd Bombardment Wing which, in 1953, had a detachment deployed in the UK. (Artwork by Tom Cooper)

To replace the ageing RB-29 in the strategic reconnaissance role, starting in 1949 the USAF acquired RB-50s in three different configurations. All converted from B-50s, these were standardised as the RB-50E (14 for photo reconnaissance and observation), RB-50F (14 with the SHORAN radar navigation system and deployed for mapping, charting, and geodetic surveys) and RB-50G (15 for electronic gathering). RB-50Gs had a crew of 16 and were primarily operated by the 55th SRW (1950–1954) and by the 91st SRW (1949–1951). This artwork shows RB-50G serial 47-143, named *Little Red Ass*. On 29 July 1953, while assigned to the 91st SRS, and operated from Yokato AB in Japan, the aircraft was shot down by Soviet interceptors, with the loss of 16 out of 17 crewmembers. (Artwork by Tom Cooper)

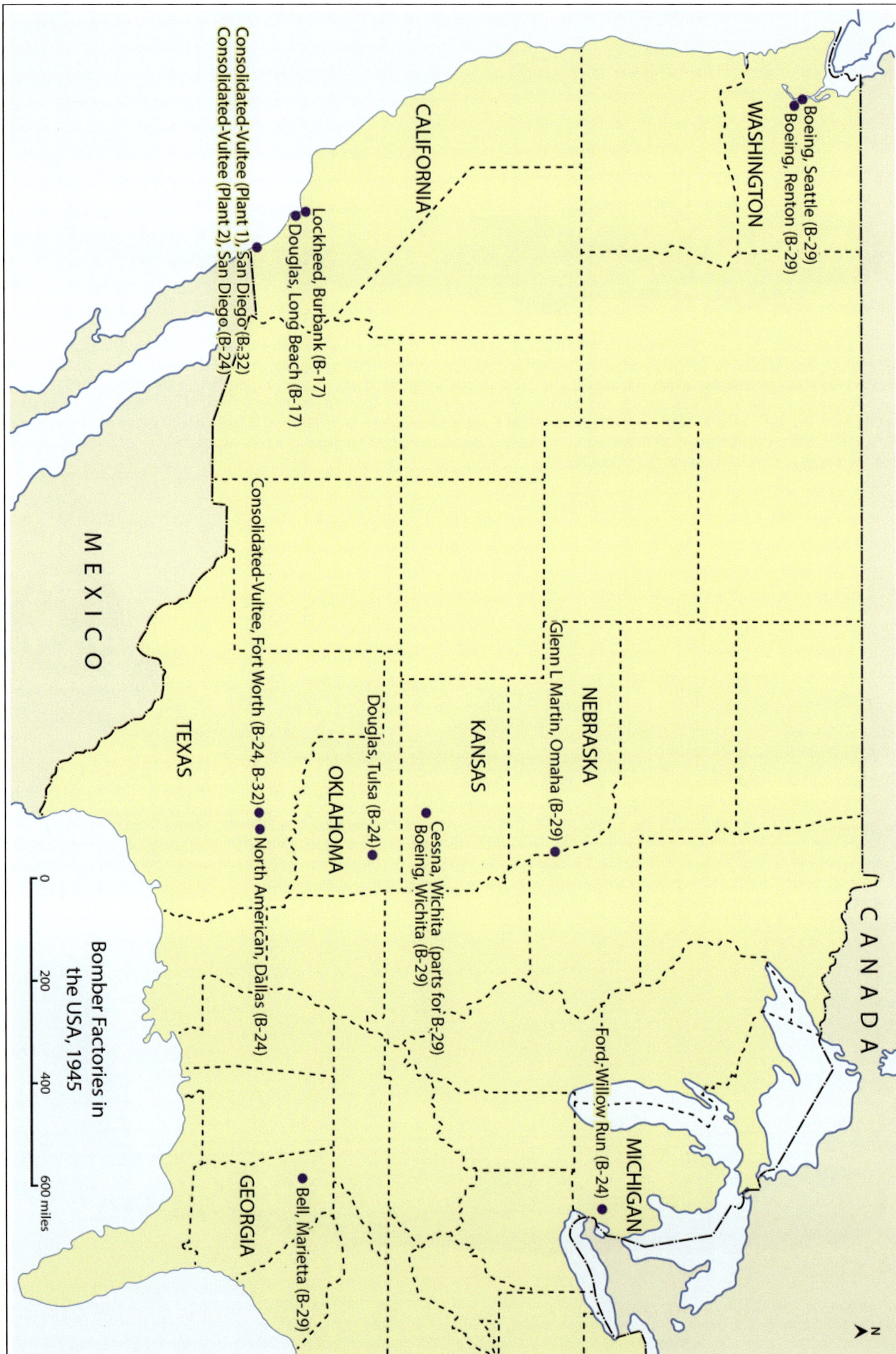

Major US bomber factories in 1945. (Map by George Anderson)

Taking lessons learned during his work on the Lockheed Vega, in 1930 Jack Northrop produced the Alpha mail-plane of which only 17 were built with some going to the USAAC and a few to the Chinese Nationalist Air Force. (Northrop)

worked as chief engineer on the Vega, a small, high-wing monoplane favoured by aviatrix Amelia Earhart in addition to Wiley Post, but in 1929 he developed a monoplane with engine buried in the fuselage and with twin tail booms. It was his first step toward a flying wing, a streamlined and low drag concept with which he became obsessed.

It was in this year that Jack Northrop set up the Avion Company with Ken Jay but this lasted less than a year before it had to sell to United Aircraft and Transport Corporation (UATC), which had itself formed on 1 February 1929 under a partnership between Boeing Airplane Company and Pratt & Whitney. UATC went on a buying spree, purchasing the Hamilton Propeller Company, the Stearman Aircraft Company and the Sikorsky Aviation Company as it pushed forward with securing airline routes across the United States in the stiff winds of opposition from competing rival groups.

In 1932, two years after selling Avion to UATC, Donald Douglas backed Jack Northrop in setting up another company, the Northrop Corporation, registered in El Segundo, California. Douglas recognised his creative genius and the two men had a similar passion for perfected aeronautical design concepts, including the flying wing with a clean, low drag aerofoil and no tail, the central section housing cockpit and internal bomb or payload capacity with few or no protuberances.

During his tenure, Northrop contributed to the Gamma and the Delta aircraft, both of which figured in aviation records of the time. A Gamma, named *Polar Star*, was used during the 1934 expedition to the Antarctic by Lincoln Ellsworth while other examples were used for unique expeditions and for breaking records, one being used for such a purpose by Howard Hughes. Taking the basic design principles behind the Gamma, Jack Northrop adapted it into a commercial transport aircraft and as such the Delta was a limited success with the Royal Canadian Air Force which used it for reconnaissance duties.

The company had difficulties with the labour unions and it was dissolved in 1937, followed two years later by its El Segundo facility becoming a subsidiary of Douglas Aircraft. Along with aviation businessman Moye Stephens, in 1939 Jack Northrop formed another company named the Northrop Corporation and set up a factory at Hawthorne, California. Jack Northrop's fortunes changed dramatically after information from the British about their ground-breaking work with the development of air-interception radar prompted a request for radar-equipped night fighters from which he developed the design for the P-61 Black Widow which first flew in May 1942.

Jack Northrop never gave up his dream of a flying wing and made some innovative progress toward that objective with an experimental tailless design designated XP-56, utilising in its construction the relatively new magnesium metal alloy due to proclaimed shortages of aluminium. The equally experimental Pratt & Whitney liquid-cooled X-1800 engine was located in the aft section of the bullet-shaped fuselage driving a pusher propeller. Only two were built and the first flight was made in September 1943. The XP-56 was never developed but it introduced some novel ways of welding magnesium through the heliarc method using a tungsten electrode protected from contamination by an inert shielding gas.

The development of the flying wing concept saw the emergence of the XB-35, a story told in Part 2 of this volume, but the company had built a reputation among industry peers by the extraordinary performance of the P-61 which is covered in Volume 1. After the war,

A development of the Northrop Gamma, the YA-13 attack aircraft was test flown in 1933 but it needed a more powerful engine, resulting in the XA-16 attack aircraft seen here, albeit an unsuccessful contender for an Army contract. (Northrop)

the company delivered the last of 674 P-61s in January 1946 while still busily engaged with development work on the flying wings and reconversion of some passenger and cargo aircraft. Northrop had also produced 14 N3PBs, 400 Vultee Vengeance dive bombers, 1,309 sets of tail surfaces and 1,291 sets of nacelles and cowlings for PBY5s in addition to 44,832 cowlings and 25,068 engine nacelles for the B-17.

Northrop was also in the forefront of several technology developments, in addition to the new heliarc welding concept. One of those with notable contribution was directly from the P-61 Black Widow night fighter and the effective use of the elevon, as the company explained:

> It was designed to incorporate in the Black Widow full span flaps which made it possible for the plane to land at slow, safe speeds on small landing strips under conditions of extreme low visibility, and to give the Black Widow, which was as big as a medium bomber, an unusual degree of manoeuvrability. The retractable aileron system of the Black Widow was a combination of the conventional type and four 'retractable aileron' panels linked to the aileron control system. These panels worked in unison with the ailerons. The entire system was controlled by the wheel in the cockpit. Roll was induced almost entirely by the retractable ailerons.
>
> Under flight conditions, there was an opening moment on the retractable ailerons. Were it not for the small conventional ailerons which were linked to the retractable ailerons, this opening moment would be translated into a disposition to over-balance. In other words, once the wheel was moved from the neutral position, the retractable aileron would tend to continue its travel out of the wing until fully extended. There was, naturally, a trailing moment on the small conventional aileron.
>
> This trailing moment was just great enough to overcome the opening moment of the retractable ailerons and to impart 'feel' to the system. As the speed of the airplane increased, the opening moment on the retractable ailerons and likewise the trailing moment on the conventional ailerons were increased. The trailing moment on the latter increased at only a slightly greater rate than did the opening moment on the retractable ailerons.
>
> As a consequence, control forces did not increase with speed in anywhere near the same proportion as did the forces of ordinary aileron systems. At high speeds, because of the fact that less force was required, the control could be moved more quickly and, hence, a more rapid rate of roll attained than was possible with the average conventional system under the same circumstances.
>
> At slow speeds with the flaps up, the effectiveness of the retractable ailerons was equal to that of the usual system. However, with the flaps down, effectiveness (as expressed in terms of rate of roll with full aileron deflection) was approximately 40 percent greater than that of the average conventional installation. In addition, the retractable ailerons retained effectiveness down to and past the stall. The ship would roll from side to side in quick response to the wheel. Likewise, the ship could be held straight during a stall with one engine wind-milling, while the other was at take-off power.

By the end of the decade Northrop was at a peacetime peak with 7,500 employees working on production of the F-89 Scorpion and the C-125 Raider light assault transport which made its first flight on 1 August 1949. Research activity progressed, with the tiny X-4 which test pilot Charles Ticker had taken into the air on 15 December 1948. Control of this tailless research aircraft was through elevons on the trailing edge of the swept wing but overall the performance was disappointing and only two were built.

But research and innovative design was at the heart of the company's philosophy and efforts were made to enter the missile field and it was also engaged in nuclear research by way of radiation shielding for nuclear-powered aircraft. Monte Carlo methods were used with high-capacity electronic computers and a prosthesis laboratory designed a light but heavy-duty artificial limb known as the Northrop Simplex Arm. Oliver P Echols joined Northrop in 1949 as chairman, succeeding Richard W Millar who had been appointed to that position only a year earlier.

As the decade closed, Northrop faced potential collapse, with losses of $3.8 million in the year ending 31 July 1949. This loss was largely built up after writing off funds in development of a three-engine commercial transport and with a loss of $4.4 million on a fixed-price contract to the military for production of the C-125. With orders flagging, prospects for the company were believed to hinge on the flying wings, notably the YB-49 but on 15 March 1950 the programme was cancelled, along with Jack Northrop's hope of delivering a flying wing bomber which could outfly any of its conventional competitors. At least for the next 25 years, when it would re-emerge in the guise of the B-2, a highly classified design which Jack Northrop was allowed to see in model form before he died on 18 February 1981.

3

WEAPONS AND WAR PLANS

The US strategic bombing campaign of the Second World War was a template for the core function of the post-war, independent Air Force. Planning for that began on 4 August 1945, two days before the atomic bomb was dropped on Hiroshima, when the Joint Strategic Survey Committee (JSSC) and the Joint War Plans Committee (JWPC) requested the Joint Staff Planners (but abbreviated to JPS) to put together a strategic plan for US military roles and responsibilities worldwide after the war. First, it was necessary to get scientific and technical advice on just what weapons might be available to the post-war military and when they might conceivably be deployed.

They consulted with Major General Leslie Groves, who had directed the Manhattan Project developing the atomic bomb, and Dr Vannevar Bush, chairman of the Joint Committee on New Weapons and Equipment. A noted engineer and patent-holder, Dr Bush had been running the Office of Scientific Research and Development (OSRD) since 1941 and had administered the atomic bomb project. Dr Bush met with the JPS on 22 August to give his opinion on what weapons might be available and how that might influence planning for strategic bases. It was as important in the planning stage to define the type and capabilities of weapons concerned so as to estimate the location of operating and support bases.

Implicit within the debate was consideration of the newly developed long-range ballistic missile and how that might affect procurement and deployment of conventional aircraft, be they piston or jet powered. Dr Bush said that he did not believe that rockets with a range much greater than that of the V2, 200 miles (322km) or thereabouts, would be possible in the near future but that even if missiles with a range of 2,000 miles (3,220km) were possible, the US would still need foreign bases from which to launch them.

Clearly, the atomic bomb was the more significant weapon for the post-war world and the fact that in 1945 it was not possible to envisage their size being sufficiently small to allow deployment in guns or torpedoes. Dr Bush concluded that the manned aircraft was the only means by which atomic weapons could be a significant development in US strategic thinking. But he was less imaginative than the scientific and technical capabilities of his contemporaries in weapons development, who would deliver such applications for operational deployment within 10 years. By which time, as we saw in Chapter 1, the concept of the strategic bomber had become entrenched in doctrine.

For his part, General Groves concurred with Dr Bush regarding the uniqueness of atomic weapons and reflected that the United States needed to plan a global deployment of bases for the next 50 to 100 years from which the aircraft could operate against multiple threats. But he was more optimistic regarding long-range guided missiles, which he believed could be possible within 10–20 years. However, both men shared the opinion that there was no defence against the atom bomb other than to shoot down the aircraft which was carrying it.

Dr Bush was more confident that, even with atomic weapons possessed by two opposing sides, a first-strike posture was no longer necessary because after an initial attack the response could be unleashed if the weapons were kept underground and protected from destruction. In effect, he asserted the idea that battles are won by weapons while wars are won by economics; the more robustly the supply-side could replenish destroyed stocks of bombs, tanks and guns the less it would lose through attrition. It followed therefore that the erosion of the aggressor's production capacity would tip the balance in favour of the defendant's ability to prevail. When asked about those reserve stocks of atomic bombs, Groves was less forthcoming, perhaps for the reason that (as discussed in a previous chapter) stocks were in fact almost non-existent.

The JPS submitted its statement on future US military policy to the Joint Chiefs on 30 August, followed by a plan for the employment of US forces on 9 October. Within eight days they had both been accepted and approved. The Chiefs saw world peace as the post-war goal of the US military, forces so strong, capable and ready that no other nation would challenge them by starting a war of aggression, seeing the Soviet Union as potentially the most uncertain of wartime allies in a post-war world. Britain was considered to be the third strongest, most capable and important power and one which would remain closest to the United States. But it was not just major wars for which the military must be ready to act. In its mandatory role as defined by Congress, the armed services would have to act on behalf of the United Nations and be prepared to put out any brushfire that flared up in peacetime, if called upon to do so.

Portent of a changed world as Allied military leaders accompany each other on a tour of Berlin after the German surrender. General Bernard Montgomery (centre) is accompanied by Russia's Marshal Zhukov with the remains of the Brandenburg Gate in the background. (NARA)

In the closing months of 1945 the JWPC gathered together relevant bodies to prepare a joint war plan for the United States to provide a range of actions the United States could conduct in the event of conflict with the Soviet Union in the next three years. Events in the first months of 1946 appeared to signal an urgency to complete that work and on 2 March the first draft of such a plan was presented to the JPS. Assessments of Soviet military strength invoked a sense of grim foreboding, estimates putting 51 Soviet divisions in Germany and Austria, 20 divisions in Poland, 50 divisions in the Near and Middle East and 20 divisions in Hungary and Yugoslavia.

The first attempt to provide a war plan in the event of conflict began on 2 March 1946 when the JWPC distributed a discussion paper which was completed on 13 April providing several different studies indicating the number of occupation forces required for Europe and the Middle East and for deployment to the Far East together with a list of air bases required. This study was named PINCHER and did not specifically identify the initial use of atomic weapons due to their scarcity at this date but it acknowledged that they could be critical in any future war. As sent to the JPS, it was the basis for a Joint Basic War Plan which interleaved with similar plans from the Army and the Navy. It was approved for basic planning on 18 June.

During this period and very shortly thereafter, significant intelligence was available that the Soviet Union was beginning a process of infiltration into Middle Eastern states and that there was a probability that Russia would seek allies in that area. It was known that for historical reasons, Russia had always wanted access to the Mediterranean Sea by way of the Sea of Marmara and that

In charge of the overall management of America's atomic bomb project, General Leslie Groves (right) chats to physicist Robert Oppenheimer who led the scientists that made possible the first detonation on 16 July 1945 at Alamogordo, New Mexico. (Department of Energy)

Critical to success in Europe and with the war against Japan, Curtis LeMay was well qualified to take charge of Strategic Air Command at a time when it was failing to satisfy requirements for the US war plan. (USAF)

disillusioned Arab countries were vulnerable to Soviet offers of cooperation and collaboration leading to Russian bases in those territories. It was for this reason among several that there was a distinct concern over the places American bombers would have to attack in the event of war.

What was possible in any war would hinge on the availability of weapons and on their demonstrated performance on test or from experience in previous conflicts. Atomic weapons were at the heart of a strategic bomber force and yet there was no realistic understanding of just what they could do to different targets involving different materials under different situations. In deciding that the atom bomb was at the core of a strike capability, the only way to understand their potential was to conduct a weapons-effects analysis and that meant testing them against calibrated targets. The first real proposal for which can be traced back to 25 August 1945, just prior to the Japanese surrender, when Senator Brian McMahon declared that to test these weapons against naval vessels he would 'like to see these Japanese naval ships taken to sea and an atomic bomb dropped on them'.

A more nuanced reason was expressed by General Arnold on 18 September when he suggested to the Joint Chiefs that such a collection of ships be assembled for a scientific test which could also determine the future requirements of marine architects as to ship design requirements for survival in an age of atomic warfare. Navy Admiral Ernest King supported that idea and on 16 October backed up Arnold's suggestion and the JPS was assigned the task of planning such an exercise involving two bombs tested on different days and for different analyses. The JPS handed the job to Major General Curtis LeMay and that was approved by the Chiefs on 28 December and by President Truman on 10 January 1946.

Navy support for this test was driven by the stated reason but also as a means of testing the veracity of exaggerated claims about the effectiveness of atomic weapons. The Air Force magnified its justification for carrying the strategic role through untested statements about the way they could destroy targets and the Navy was suspicious of these claims. Navy supporters in the Pentagon wanted to gather data which would argue the case for a sustainable maritime force in the nuclear era. They had been here before when, in 1921 bombers had tried to destroy ships with inconclusive results for long-term viability. Those tests had been a mechanism for attempts by the then Army Air Service to supplant the Navy's battleships by demonstrating that they were unlikely to survive in an age of air warfare.

When plans were discussed for what would be known as OPERATION CROSSROADS, opposition for the tests came from scientists already concerned at the environmental impact, several claiming that the water around the Bikini Atoll test site in the Marshall Islands would be a 'witch's brew' of toxic radiation. With 167 residents moved from the atoll, 95 redundant warships and smaller boats were placed inside the lagoon together with a wide and diverse range of animals including 5,000 rats and 500 mice, pigs and goats to provide data for the National Cancer Institute.

Designated Able and with personnel removed to at least 11.8 miles (19km) from the site, the first Mk III bomb was dropped by a B-29 (*Dave's Dream*) piloted by General Roger M Ramsey commanding the 58th Bombardment Wing (BW) on 1 July 1946 local date. The explosion occurred at a height of 550ft (167m) but 2,000ft (610m) off the planned target due to wind affecting the fall of the descending package. The effects were less than those predicted, largely due to the missed target which was directly over the battleship *Nevada*, which suffered minor damage from blast pressure on casings. The second detonation on 25 July named Baker was from a device moored 900ft (274m) below a Navy landing ship which was completely vapourised. Nine of 20 ships moored within 2,600ft (792m) of the zero point sank or capsized and these included the battleship *Arkansas* and the carrier *Saratoga*.

A third test planned for a deeper detonation named Charlie was cancelled but the results of Able and Baker were significant in providing assessment of the type and nature of damage incurred at varying distances from the zero point. Damage to the ships from Baker was due largely to the propagated shock wave but the greatest surprise was the level of radiation, which affected more than 90 percent of the entire target area. The enormous resources required to carry out these tests chafed with General Groves, who opposed any further tests so that his teams could concentrate on bomb production.

The final report of the CROSSROADS tests published on 30 June 1947 included results from the detailed analysis of the effects on Hiroshima and Nagasaki and with the four site evaluations it concluded that the weapon was one primarily suited for use against people and 'large urban and industrial areas', noting that 'The Bikini tests would strongly suggest that ships under way will rarely constitute targets for atomic bomb attack'. There was concern too about the radiation effects and the information from these four detonations made sombre reading for the consequences of using such weapons on the battlefield.

A group of senior nuclear physicists who provided a US leadership in atomic weapons for four crucial years before Russia acquired its own bomb, a period during which the Russians were aware of the threat that the American lead posed. (Department of Energy)

The inevitability of having to face these was expressed very early after the Second World War. On 26 July 1946 the Joint Chiefs of Staff noted that 'In a war with the USSR we must envisage complete and total hostilities unrestricted in any way on the Soviet part', emphasising that 'preparations envisaged on our part and plans must be on this basis'. They were convinced that 'gas, bacteriological warfare, and atomic weapons will be used'. It was this assumption that underpinned JCS 1725/1 which defined the war plan as envisaged in February 1947 but, paradoxically, the Chiefs believed that a response to such Soviet attack must use only conventional weapons, the document defining that 'The outline plan has been prepared on the conservative assumption that weapons of mass destruction, such as the atomic bomb, will not be used by the United States and its allies'. At this date only the United States had atomic bombs.

Concern at this implication, that the US would not use its atomic weapons in a shooting war, moved Army Chief of Staff Dwight Eisenhower to change the wording when he argued that contrary to JCS 1725/1 there was in fact 'considerable probability, if not a certainty, that atomic weapons would be used in any such war'. On 30 April the Chiefs changed their position and amended the document to include such atomic weapons as were available. Previously, war plans had been tailored to two different doctrines. In short, two schools of thought about nuclear energy and nuclear weapons had emerged in the United States immediately after the Second World War. One believed that America had the monopoly on the atom bomb and should retain it so that it could be used to constrain Soviet hegemony. The other group believed that another country would eventually get the bomb and that it could never be a unilateral monopoly of the United States.

Planning Armageddon

As early as 7 January 1946 the US set up a Committee on Atomic Energy to submit recommendations to the UN Atomic Energy Commission, which was founded later that month. Known as the Acheson-Lilienthal Report, it was submitted to the US State Department on 16 March and proposed that fissile material should be under international control, thus preventing any one nation accumulating sufficient stock to make a bomb, that the US should abandon its monopoly and share its secrets with the Russians in return for an international agreement not to conduct tests but also that the Russians should desist from making a bomb of its own. When it went before the UN on 14 June 1946 the Russians could not agree that the United States retain the bomb until an international agreement came into force and in December the idea was rejected.

Further work under PINCHER produced several separate plans for different global sectors and on 16 July 1947 the JWPC informed the JPS that it was ready to prepare a combined warfighting plan for conflict with the Soviet Union. These plans were adjusted over time to input the changing capabilities of SAC aircraft, bombs and flight planning, factors which controlled what could be done in an atomic war and what could be conducted in a strategic conflict involving both nuclear and conventional weapons.

Between 1945 and 1949 the medium, heavy and very-heavy bomber categories would change due to the introduction of the

Much publicised, the dramatic image of the Operation CROSSROADS Baker test on 24 July 1946 at Bikini Atoll. (US Department of Energy)

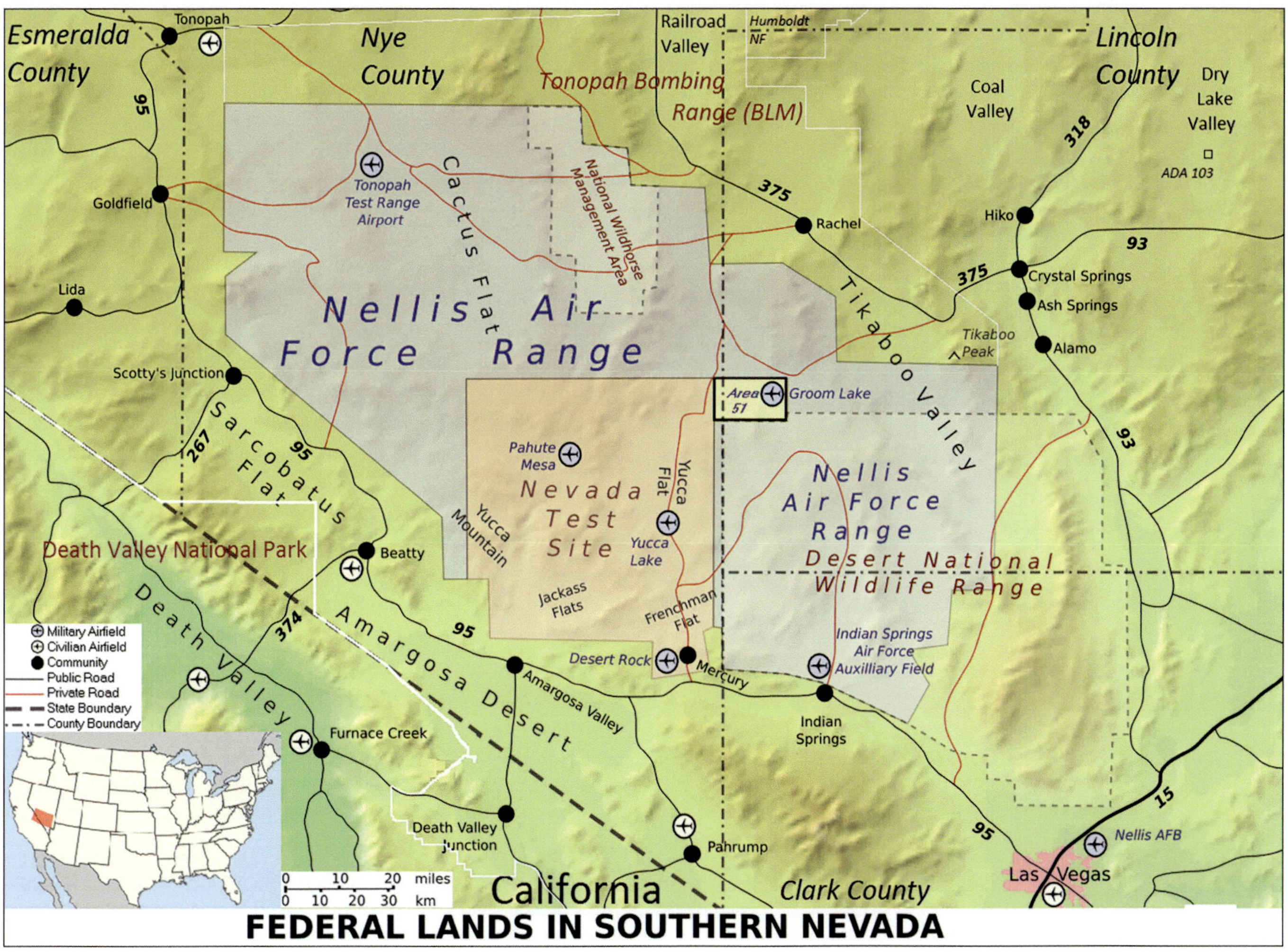

A map of the area where nuclear tests were conducted in Nevada, a location embracing Area 51 where many Top Secret engineering and technology projects were developed and a region in which experimental programmes evolved. (Finlay McWalter)

B-50 and the B-36 in 1948 and the imminent availability of the all-jet B-47 when it made its first flight in December 1947. Moreover, during 1948 Air Materiel Command had requested that Boeing's successor to the B-36 be powered by jet engines.

During the PINCHER studies, the Assistant Chief of the Air Staff for Plans (AC/AS-5) began to develop a strategic plan for how all the various assets of the Air Force would be utilised and integrated in a future war. It wanted a high-level plan it could pull out of a drawer to instantly mobilise at the onset of conflict all the various elements, commands, units, bases, equipment, munitions and personnel required. Although the specific detail on how such an integrated force could be best utilised would rely on just what the conditions were, it allowed flexible options down interconnecting chains of command.

Named MAKEFAST, the plan was based on tried and tested plans from the Second World War and focused on a strategic bombing campaign against petroleum resources and on refining and distribution of fuel, without specific reference to targeted population centres or major cities. The rationale followed a logical flow path that believed in a modern military, warfighting machine, rather than one assembled purely for defence, would be quickly neutralised if it had no fuel. Moreover, to achieve a given result, the tonnage of bombs dropped on these facilities would be less than that for rail networks, marshalling yards or power plants. It would also be completed without resort to atomic bombs, which could be held in reserve for the final denouement, in which regard it closely followed the logic employed in the final years of the Pacific war against Imperial Japan.

The fluid nature of MAKEFAST required continual updating and Spaatz requested a new version, completed in February 1947 and named EARSHOT, further modified to EARSHOT JUNIOR

The J47 turbojet engine significantly raised the performance of the B-36 and, as shown here, provided propulsion for the B-47 which was emerging at the close of the 1940s as a replacement for the B-29 and the B-50. (NARA)

Atomic tests were supported by a wide range of measurement equipment including Kytoon balloons, as seen here at Indian Springs AFB before release for meteorological data-gathering. (Author's archive)

that summer, under which SAC developed its first formal plan for a strategic atomic attack on the Soviet Union. That was named Operation Plan OPLAN 14-47. By this time the JWPC had decided that sufficient work had already been done to justify a concentrated plan for attacks on the Soviet Union within the next three years and this was authorised on 29 August 1947 by the JSPC which on enactment of the National Security Act had replaced the Joint Staff Planners. It carried the codename BROILER and assumed the use of atomic weapons from the outset.

The JSPC asked the Joint Strategic Plans Group (JSPG) to expand the remit and include a situation where Western Europe had been overrun by Soviet forces and that a military response had no political constraints. That moved the study to suggest an all-out strategic campaign designed to remove Russian troops from all territories it occupied after 1939 and its attack on Poland. This was an important step in air-fighting strategies because it included the defence of Western Europe, where previously it had conducted strategies based exclusively in an attack on the Soviet territories, interpreting the requirement as a confrontation with Russia.

This initially had been coded as JWPC 486/7 and would embrace much of what had been derived through PINCHER with the primary thrust up through Turkey and the Balkan countries into Soviet Russia rather than through Western Europe, which had been assumed to be under Soviet occupation including the UK. The change to an atomic-inclusive attack was new, however. In a significant change from strategies during the Second World War, where the Army Air Force had emphasised its priority on targeted bombing, in reality it was area bombing that became the pattern in the closing year of the war in Europe. Under BROILER, for the first time, area bombing was considered both acceptable and at the core of its strategy and cities became targets.

A typical scene displaying the new Air Force as SAC introduced its B-47 and prepared for an all-jet force in an age of high-performance aircraft. (USAF)

But there was uncertainty. Without a political objective, either for the defeat of the Soviet military in the field, the total eradication of the Russian nation state, or merely the destruction of the Soviet industrial war-making infrastructure, there was no defined end-game in the BROILER plan. That compromised its effectiveness as a tool because it ignored the reality of conflict, that wars in general are started by politicians, ordering the military into action, and ended by diplomats, negotiating peace agreements signed off by the politicians who started them. Without those beginning and end definitions as to cause and goals there could be no means and wherefores as to how it would proceed and to what purpose.

Unlike PINCHER, BROILER embraced the destruction of civil infrastructure through a lack of intelligence as to precisely where in a vast urban sprawl the 'military' complex was situated; atomic weapons would have to be used in an attack on the city itself. The need for accurate information was compromised due to the decline in intelligence-gathering resources about the geography of the USSR, the number of reconnaissance aircraft at SAC having been reduced from 55 in January 1947 to 24 by September. Through BROILER, the outflow of collateral advantage from using atomic weapons began to take hold. It dawned on planners that if a whole city became a legitimate target, the population of workers themselves became a military target and the Air Force Intelligence Directorate posed the question: 'What was a city besides a collection of industry?'

There was now an advantage in the massive damage zone after the detonation of an atomic bomb in that it could create a very large psychological and demoralising reaction in the survived population, hampering deployment of human resources to cope with the attack. The myth that the destructive bombing of cities and large inhabited areas could disconnect the group from the national will by severing morale and causing an anti-establishment revolt is specious at best and yet to be experienced in any war in which the general public come under attack. For some inexplicable reason, that belief was very strong during all war plans and attack strategies in this period.

Theorists would argue this issue for many years and George Kennan, noted diplomatist and supporter of the doctrine of 'containment' rather than 'confrontation', observed that 'all you will do is convince them that we are barbarians trying to destroy their way of life'. But staff planners were more nuanced and LeMay was supportive of city attacks on the basis that if the bombers were significantly off-target, the atom bombs would do certain damage to other aspects of the Soviet war effort. This was an important point at the time when SAC crews were miserably deficient in even the expected standards of accuracy.

Presented on 8 November 1947, BROILER satisfied JWPC 486/7 but it was disturbingly ahead of the resources it would need to draw upon. The sheer scale of the undertaking, whatever the ultimate objective, was far beyond the men and the machines available when it envisaged use of atomic weapons from the outset in a war theorised to begin in 1948. It would begin, said the theorists, with bombing strikes delivered from bases in the United States, the UK and the Middle East, with 34 atomic bombs dropped on 24 cities.

Seven would be dropped on Moscow, three on Leningrad, two on Kharkov and Stalingrad and single bombs on other cities. Overall, it assumed availability of 100–200 atomic bombs when not even half that number would be available by mid-1948. But the lack of information about the number of bombs available made any assessment of capability problematic. Moreover, the planners worked on paper requirements for crew capabilities, performance and bombing accuracy and those were far from realistic.

When BROILER planners drafted their strategies, only the B-29 and the B-50 were available. The B-36 was not yet entering

SAC and with all the uncertainties of a major new undertaking, its performance and capabilities were unknown and estimates at best. By the end of 1947, SAC had only 32 aircraft capable of carrying the atomic bomb and 20 percent of Soviet targets were beyond the range of even the closest air bases.

The solution was to fly one-way missions which, however distasteful, was justified pragmatically by Major General Earl Partridge when he proposed to 'Expend the crew, expend the bomb, expend the airplane all at once. Kiss them goodbye and let them go', and when reflecting on that decision, admitting that it was 'a pretty cold blooded point of view', conceding that he 'believed that it is economically best for the country'. Not all were that brutal in their judgement, General Powers believing that the crewmembers 'are not stupid…they might change plans many times along the way'.

Of primary concern was the level of attrition due to Soviet air defences, where large quantities of German anti-aircraft artillery in the form of guns and rockets, supplemented by jet-powered fighters, could severely disrupt expectations of getting the bombers through in sufficient numbers to achieve a result. The Soviet PVO (*Protivo Vosdushnaya Oborono Strany*) air defence system included 1,600 fighters, a considerable percentage of which were jet-powered, threatening the ponderous bombers on their way into denied airspace, over the target and during the return leg. Concerns about advancing Russian capabilities with air defence radar were justified by the amount of German equipment captured at the end of the war and put to use in an integrated defence system.

BROILER had begun to swing the pendulum of defence back across to Western Europe, a vector contested by some who felt that a direct attack on the Soviet Union rather than defence of recently defeated countries should be the priority. But events in Eastern Europe, including a communist coup in Czechoslovakia and problems brewing over Berlin, shifted the focus of attention. Army commanders were concerned that any attempt to defeat Russia from the south was bound to fail if the entire northern continent was in Soviet hands, threatening to cut off access via the Mediterranean and the southern route through Italy.

A Changing Landscape

International tension increased considerably during early 1948 and what became in essence a precursor move to set up a formal military alliance between friendly nations took place on 12–21 April 1948 when representatives of the US, the UK and Canada discussed in Washington DC a cooperative framework for coordinated military action. There was a need to move the focus firmly on to a coordinated international response, should Soviet political ambitions send their troops into action against the West. Known as HALFMOON, this envisaged how broad swathes of the Western world along with Middle East states would align together to defeat the Soviet Union.

A range of bases in many countries was examined as part of the expanded plan, with the expectation that if a war broke out, 1949 being the earliest date now envisaged, B-36s would fly bombing missions from the United States while B-29s and the B-50s would fly out of the UK, Cairo and Okinawa. Here again the use of atomic bombs was implicit from the outset but after a briefing on 6 May 1948, Truman raised concerns over the early use of those weapons. He was concerned about the availability of these in sufficient number to sustain an attack, and about the public acceptability of their use 'for aggressive purposes'.

The matter was raised at a National Security Council meeting on 19 May and debate ensued, followed by a resolution adopted on 16 September specifically approving their use at any time should war break out. The President had achieved his objective by stimulating a pause in the tacit assumption allowing time for a measured and considered debate. It was on this date that US warfighting policy specifically sanctioned the use of atomic weapons at any time in any conflict. Before official approval, HALFMOON planners upped the number of targets to 210, 70 of which would be major urban centres, Moscow and Leningrad specified as top priority as they had the single most concentrated industrial groupings for war production.

Targeting was shifted to give further priority to petroleum production, the top 10 refineries in Russia being hit and taken out of action in the first 70 objectives during which 72 percent of total Soviet capacity would be eliminated. SAC would use conventional attacks to destroy transportation networks, hydro-electric plants, ports and waterways, with coastal areas mined to prevent maritime movement and inhibit naval operations. For the first time in warfighting strategies, US naval power was invoked to 'supplement and support the air offensive', but in a vague and ill-defined way.

Considerable debate ensued over the relative roles of the Navy and the Air Force and these matters have been discussed elsewhere in this book. It is unclear what the Air Force expected of the Navy but the carriers and naval air strike potential was clearly an asset in any conflict, given the proximity to targets available with fleet operations. But this was a year of challenges and threats, as the geopolitical clouds darkened and the Soviets shut down access to Berlin's Western sector, precipitating an airlift of unprecedented scale that began on 26 June.

As discussed elsewhere in this book, SAC sent B-29s to the UK and to West Germany. In a move indicative of just how firm the Air Force considered HALFMOON to be, formal protests were made to the Pentagon when C-54 transport aircraft were assigned to the airlift, removing them from their Middle East deployment should war break out, compromising the transport services carrying weapons and logistics to the UK, Cairo and Okinawa. By September, 224 C-54s were committed to the airlift, 52 percent of the entire Military Air Transport Service (MATS). The initial attack on D-Day (start of operations) would come from conventional bombers on Okinawa, followed on D+15 with atomic strikes from the UK and Cairo.

The Armed Forces Special Weapons Project (AFSWP) was responsible for assembling and delivering atomic bombs to where they were needed by the Air Force, a task made more difficult by the lack of appropriate facilities at forward bases to which the B-29s would have been flown in the event of war. Special expeditionary buildings did exist for transport to overseas bases but with a significant portion of MATS aircraft assigned to the Berlin airlift, that would leave logistical and support materials in short supply at places where they would be needed. When erected, the expeditionary building for installing atomic bombs measured 20ft 6.1m) by 100ft (30.5m) in size and the extensive attention to war plans encouraged special procedures for conveying, assembling and fitting these weapons.

A major problem responsible for slowing down readiness levels at SAC was the convoluted way in which bombs would be delivered to the aircraft. All atom bombs were stored at Sandia Base, operated by the Sandia Corporation of Albuquerque, New Mexico, and the only loading site in the United States was at Kirtland AFB, New Mexico. Construction of six National Stockpile Sites (NSSs) began in 1947, with Site A adjacent to Kirtland and Sandia, Site B alongside Gray AFB, Texas, and Site C at Clarksville Base, Fort Campbell, on the Kentucky/Tennessee border, for handling the weapons for bombers. Three other NSSs were located at: Bossier Base, Barksdale,

Critical to the development of warfighting strategies, the Joint Chiefs of Staff in 1948. Front from left to right: Chief of Naval Operations Admiral Louis E Denfield; Admiral William D Leahy; Secretary of Defense James V Forrestal; Chief of Staff of the USAF General Carl Spaatz; Chief of Staff of the Army General Omar Bradley. (Department of Defense)

Louisiana; Lake Mead Base at Nellis AFB, Nevada; and Medina Base at Lakeland AFB, Texas. All were operational by the end of 1949, supplemented by seven Operational Storage Sites (OSSs). NSS and OSS facilities were controlled by the AEC and the AFSWP.

The AFSWP worked closely with Sandia Laboratories' Z-Division to develop procedures for the supply of atomic bombs. But not until 14 December 1948 in a rehearsal dubbed Operation UNLIMITED, was the process first tested by integrating the AFSWP, the AEC and the US Air Force. To handle the bombs, Special Weapons Units (SWEs) were set up each with 77 individuals on constant alert through rotation ready in an instant to deploy anywhere in the world where it would be necessary to assemble and install a bomb for flight in a B-29, a B-50 or a B-36.

But resources were limited and as of this date no SWE had a full inventory of essential equipment so cannibalising was the only way to get a single SWE functional, with the implication that there was only one place where the full sequence could be completed. A critical link in the chain was the way the AEC operated with the Air Force to deliver the bombs it legally had responsibility for, together with the speed and ease with which assembly could be completed. While the case, deployment fixtures in the bomber and control mechanisms for its arming and release were the responsibility of the Air Force, the internal construction containing the fissile materials and the method of detonation were largely classified and controlled by the AEC.

How the two bodies coordinated would be crucial to whether the war plans were valid or not, as was the way the bombs could be put together. Noted elsewhere, the Mk III was difficult to assemble and took time as well as skilled personnel. Under development at this date, the Mk IV was designed for ease of assembly and a dialled yield from 1KT to 31KT, approximately 0.7 percent to 210 percent of the yield of the uranium-235 'gun' type bomb dropped on Hiroshima. Almost the same explosive package as the Mk III, the Mk IV had production-style electrical units, a modular assembly method and better conditioning and monitoring equipment between the bomb and the aircraft carrying it. It would become available in 1949 and remain in service until 1953, about 550 being built and delivered making the Mk IV the first production-line atom bomb.

Getting the bombs to the bombers was also problematic in the situation where the AEC held control of dispersal and transportation. In any situation where SAC wanted atom bombs, aircraft would have to fly to one of the National Stockpile Sites. There, the bombs would be assembled and checked out and escorted out to the flight line where there were ramps and facilities for uploading the ordnance using a pit for locating the Mk III or Mk IV up into the forward bomb bay of either a B-29 or a B-50. These events would take several

The complexity of assembling and instrumenting atomic weapons for use in an operational context is indicated by the amount of work required for the Trinity Test on 16 July 1945. (Department of Energy)

days for each squadron, the flow of aircraft through the facility constrained by the need to avoid congestion through very limited space. Thus loaded, each bomber would then depart for dispersal bases in Canada, Greenland, England, Guam or Japan where the strike package would be put together and flight plans written up.

Accompanying the bombers, servicing and maintenance men would be escorted with security staff and guards flying in C-124As or C-97As of SAC's Strategic Support Squadrons. Originally, through Operation CHICKENPOX, C-97s were adapted for this role as mobile weapons servicing aircraft, a pressing need for which had driven the Air Force C-97 Stratofreighter programme but role-adaptation had been reduced to special removable kits for standard C-97s from MATS which would fly to one of the NSS facilities to pick up the bombs, all the associated equipment and relevant personnel.

An important part of the story of the American atomic bomb, the war plans developed for its use and the aircraft assigned to carry it was in the parlous state of the design, assembly, test and supply side of the weapon. Bombers have no functional part to play in deterrence or for providing an offensive capability in war other than to carry and drop bombs. But the provision of atomic bombs after the two were dropped on Japan is a confused story of indecision and uncertainty; indecision, as to whether they were ever going to form part of a strategic strike capability and in what numbers; uncertainty, in the way they would be integrated and operated as part of a conventional-atomic mix of deliverable ordnance.

It was because of these factors that the United States nearly lost hold on its atomic capability very quickly after the Second World War. The McMahon Act signed into law by Truman on 1 August 1946 determined that control of nuclear weapons and nuclear energy would be administered by a civilian organisation, the Atomic Energy Commission. Most notably, it prevented the transfer of information on these and related technologies to any other country, even those directly involved in the Manhattan Project. It evolved from Congressional hearings beginning in late 1945 when there was uncertainty as to whether the United States would be able to ban atomic weapons through the United Nations, a naive assumption based on a unipolar monopoly and in the mistaken belief that Russia was not already firmly committed to developing its own atom bomb.

Because of these multifarious reasons, the Manhattan Project team at the Los Alamos laboratories dispersed after the surrender of Japan and the original infrastructure built up for the development of the bomb began to decay. The largest facility, at Oak Ridge, Tennessee, supported the Y-12, an isotope separation plant, and the giant K-25 gaseous diffusion plant, both of which were critical to the development of uranium for the 'Little Boy' bomb dropped on Hiroshima on 6 August 1945. The three reactors at the Hanford Engineering Works at Richland, Washington, produced the plutonium for the 'Fat Man' implosion bomb dropped on Nagasaki three days later. Integral to both, the Los Alamos laboratories in

The Douglas C-124 Globemaster II made its first flight in 1949 and would quickly replace earlier and less efficient transport aircraft in supporting the new peacetime global role for the Air Force. (USAF)

New Mexico were the intellectual, scientific and creative core of the Manhattan Project where designs were done and tests were planned.

Immediately after the war, some work was retained for Operation CROSSROADS at Bikini Atoll but many people left and went to do other work across the United States, and some left the country to return home to Canada and the UK. Development of atomic bombs had been the product of a farsighted and creative group of scientists who had visionary concepts beyond the boundaries of known physics. As such, the two bomb types were experimental and the first five detonations between 1945 and 1946 were of that nature. Consequently, there was no precisely ordered record of what had been done and very little had been accomplished through established procedure, much of the work having been intuitive and one-of-a-kind.

Without descriptive notes, handbooks or manuals, the dispersion of personnel left voids in the development path and future historians would only be able to go so far in fully understanding the work that had gone on there. Many of the scientists and engineers believed they had been working for a single, specific purpose, which was to end the war quickly, and only a few had any view regarding the future possession of such weapons or of their employment as tools for conflict or even for complex war plans. It is astonishing to recall that the decision over which type of atomic bomb to develop depended largely on the knowledge that remained intact after the war regarding how to build each one. There was for a time, concern that the remaining personnel might have to opt for use of the uranium bomb, which was less efficient, because people could not be found to explain how to build the plutonium type.

The conclusion of the June 1947 report into Operation CROSSROADS determined that 'the loss of atomic dominance might be fatal to our nation and can be retained only by unflagging effort to hold that leadership in science and engineering which made the atomic bomb possible'. Concluding that in a world unlikely to build 'guarantees of permanent peace, the manufacture and stockpiling of atomic weapons and fissionable materials' had to be continued and in quantities that would 'overwhelm swiftly any potential enemy'. Thus far, four of the five atomic detonations had provided effects analyses covering blast, thermal energy and radiation. With war plans expanding, potential threats of conflict with the Soviet Union and new and significantly more capable bombers entering the inventory, it was decided to conduct the first in a series of bomb development tests.

SANDSTONE and OFFTACKLE

The Air Force wanted bigger bombs with higher yields but there was limited availability of fissionable materials and it was believed that it would be more efficient to build bombs with a yield of 100KT rather than 20KT. Analysis projected that 10 bombs of 20KT yield would each destroy an area of 3.4 miles^2 (8.8km^2), a total of 34 miles^2 (88km^2). Seven 100KT bombs could be produced with the same amount of fissionable material and each would destroy 10 miles^2 (25.9km^2), a net total of 70 miles^2 (181.3km^2).

Plutonium from uranium-238 was produced in three reactors at the Hanford Site and the 'Fat Man' bomb required 14lb (6.2kg) of which 21 percent was fissionable. But deterioration at that location due to decomposition and production there of an initiator (polonium-210) also fell. Uranium-235 was obtained from

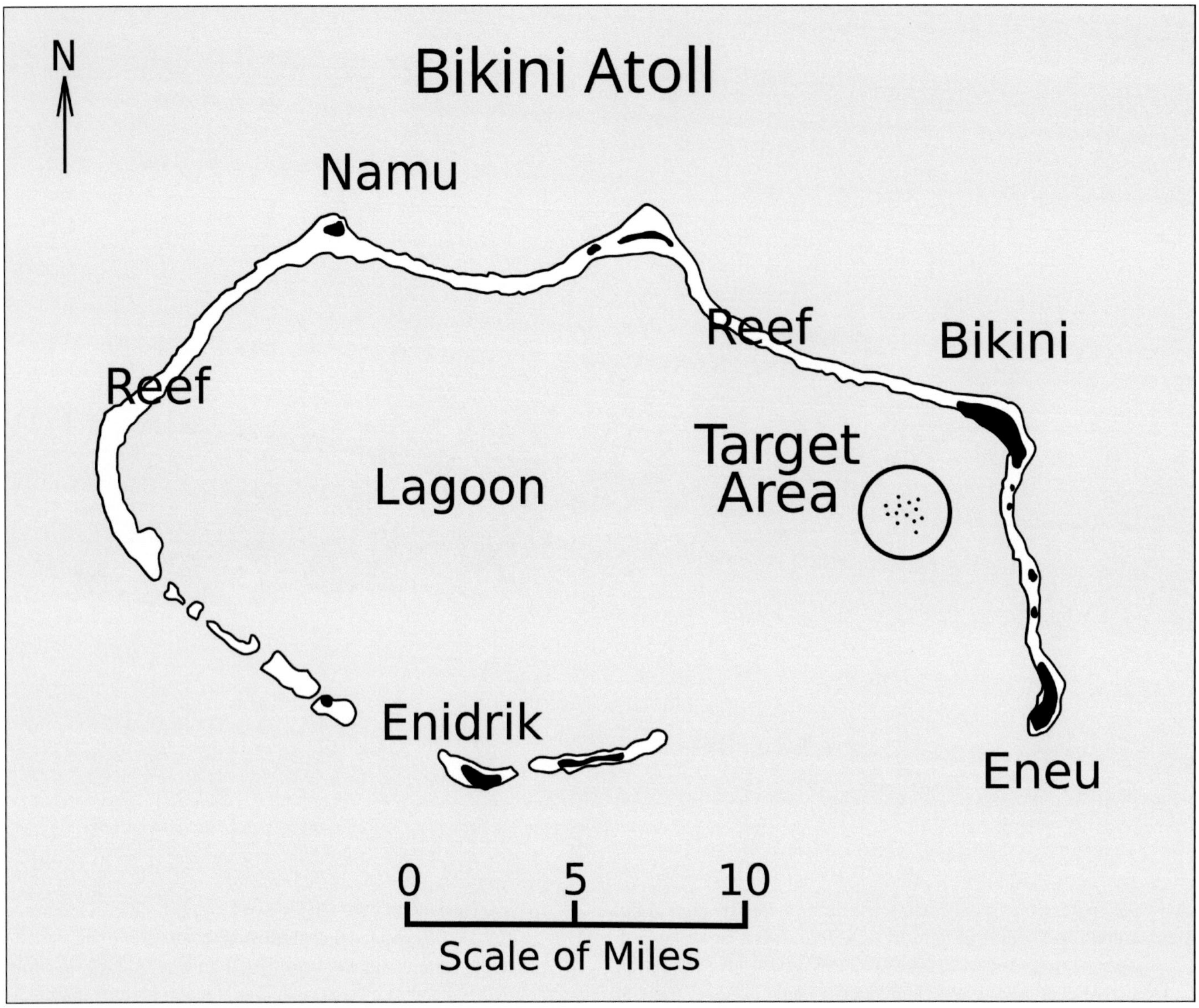

The detonation point in Bikini Atoll where the all-important Operation CROSSROADS occurred which also had the effect of informing the Russians that the United States was committed to further development of an atomic warfighting capability. (Howard Morland)

enrichment of naturally mined uranium at the Y-12 and K-25 Oak Ridge plants. This is a wasteful process and a 'Fat Man' bomb was more than 17 times as efficient as the 'Little Boy' type because it makes better use of the neutrons produced by the fission process. But one tonne of uranium ore produced eight times as much U-235 as plutonium, which was up to eight times as expensive to produce as U-235.

Several research projects provided alternative options for increasing the yield of the fission process and making better use of the available material. New ways of building initiators promised further cost-cutting solutions and technical improvements for more efficient production, assembly and operation. These needed a formal series of live tests and Truman signed off on those on 27 June 1947. This time, Los Alamos would be in charge of what were exclusively scientific and engineering evaluations under Operation SANDSTONE. The Department of Defense would be in charge of preparing the site and providing the personnel, involving 9,890 from the military together with 476 civilians.

Three detonations were conducted, on 14 April, 30 April and 14 May 1948, all with devices placed on top of 200ft (61m) towers on Eniwetak Atoll in the Marshall Islands and identified as the Pacific Proving Grounds. Powered by a 2:1 Oralloy-plutonium levitated core, the first known as X-ray had a yield of 37KT at 21 percent efficiency, the second at the Yoke test had an Oralloy core and produced a yield of 49KT, while the third on the Zebra test had a uranium core 10 percent of that in 'Fat Man' and produced a yield of 18KT.

With the potential for allowing a 63 percent increase in the number of available bombs and a 75 percent increase in yield, the Zulu device was used for the Mk IV which went into immediate production from 1949. Manufacture of the Mk III was stopped, the breakthrough had been achieved, and work had already begun on the Mk V bomb weighing little more than 3,000lb (1,360kg) compared to 10,000lb (4,536kg) for the Mk III and predecessors. Further development would get that down to 2,500lb (1,134kg) with selectable yields from 6KT to 100KT. There was now the potential for several hundred bombs and the possibility of that played into the war games and theoretical analyses which would influence revisions to existing war plans.

The advancement of engineering atom bomb technology ran counter to the provisions on hand for getting the bombs to their targets, for there was even difficulty organising the movement of these weapons to the necessary bases. During the SANDSTONE trials evaluation, the Berlin crisis precipitated the airlift and the

Surface effects from an atomic test were crucial to planning warfighting requirements in the atomic age, as here where a high-speed film image shows the base surge from the Operation CROSSROADS detonation. (Department of Energy)

aforesaid difficulties tying up MATS transport aircraft. Under plans in existence in 1948, it was not possible to load an atom bomb into a B-29, fly it across the United States and deliver it to a forward base. But partially assembled bombs could be moved up in that way and that involved a forward-deployed assembly team to take the parts and put them together. But there were still difficulties. As late as April 1950 a classified briefing identified the need for 8,000ft (2,438m) long runways for a B-29 or B-50 to take-off carrying an atomic bomb and there were very few places in the world where they were available.

With the SANDSTONE tests having delivered verification of the practicalities of the Mk IV and Mk V atom bomb being imminently available, in January 1949 an update to HALFMOON was delivered under the sub-code TROJAN. With a greater number of city targets now included, it assumed that more allies would be involved, diversifying the range of operating bases and increasing the number of targets that could be hit by expanding the places where the bombers could operate from.

Planners now envisaged 147 bombs dropped on 70 cities with the first hits on D+9, six days earlier than the basic HALFMOON plan. B-29s and B-50s from the UK, Cairo and Okinawa would carry out the initial atomic attacks and follow through with conventional raids while the B-36s would fly from Alaska. At last the optimised requirement from the war planners matched the anticipated, accelerated production plan with Mk IV bombs and there were sufficient forward assembly teams capable of being deployed worldwide to accomplish that.

When shown to Eisenhower in his role as acting Chief of the General Staff, the minimal attention paid to establishing a large US presence in Europe gave the architects of this approach inadequate understanding of the required bridgehead to halt Soviet land armies. Eisenhower wanted minimal attention to holding the Middle East and a greater focus on using SAC and the strategic bomber force to effect a push through from the Western Mediterranean and he requested revisions on 25 February 1949. In response, the JSPC ordered a revised plan with these factors at the forefront and ordered a new strategy which began work on 1 July and delivered the result on 8 November with approval by the JCS on 8 December. It was known as OFFTACKLE.

The definition of requirements began with meetings between US, British and Canadian representatives held from 26 September to 4 October 1949 in which a political definition of objectives from the Truman administration shaped what was necessary. In November 1948 the National Security Council had declared through NSC

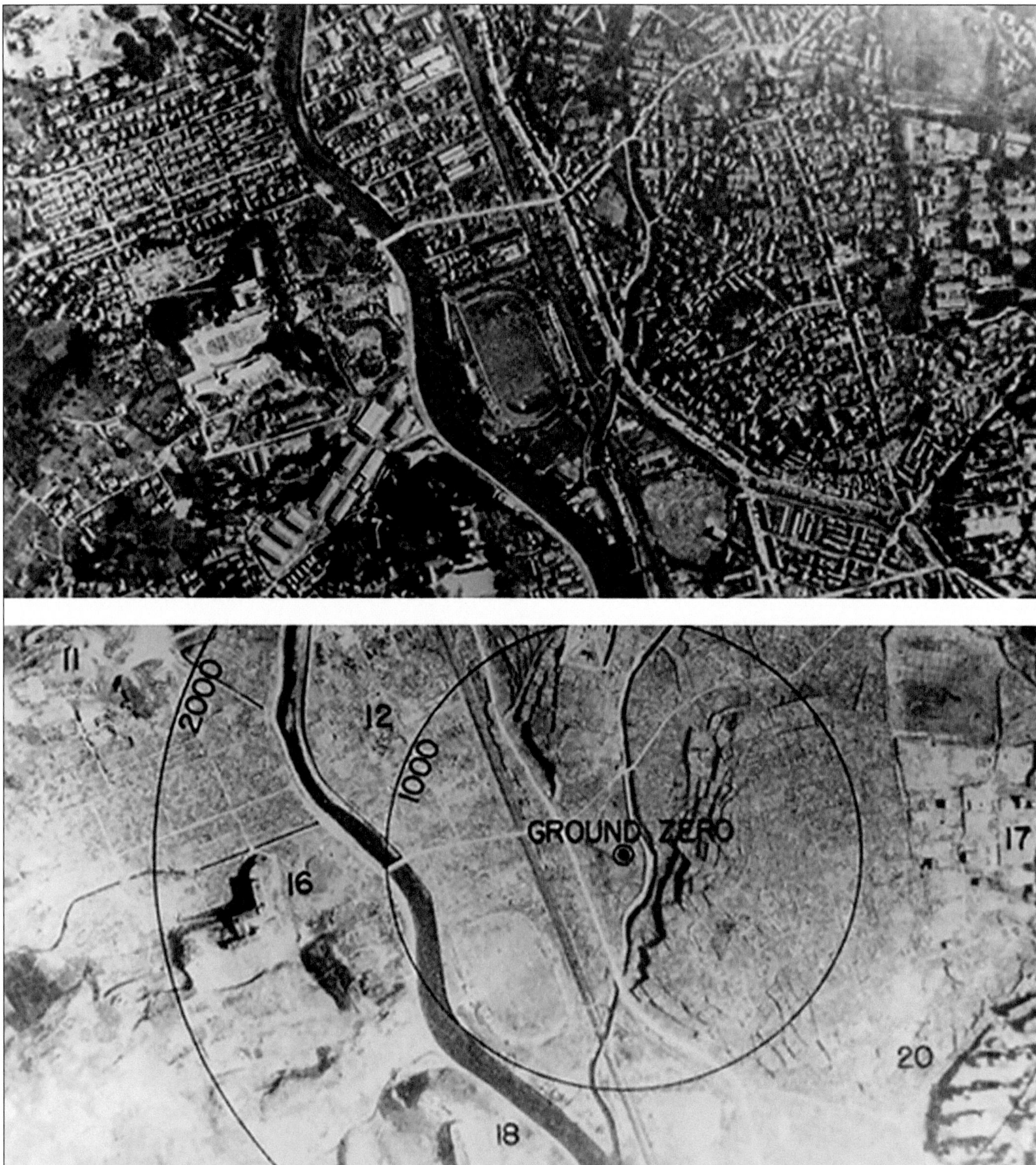

Understanding how best to use atomic weapons in a future war was informed by a bomb damage assessment after the two atomic weapons had been dropped on Japan, here showing aerial views of the city of Nagasaki, before (above) and after. (USAF)

20/4 a mandate for US forces to destroy Soviet capabilities to wage war. But it was not to deconstruct Soviet society and decapitate the leadership through instruments of war, as had previously been the objective from PINCHER to TROJAN. For the first time, military planners were given political objectives for how to begin a war with both conventional and atomic weapons with the predetermined aim of destroying Soviet military infrastructure.

Intelligence gave indications that the Russians might have up to 30 atomic weapons and that the fall of China to communist rule under Mao Zedong would greatly expand the need for a global response, with the same emphasis on strategic defence in Asia so that it could buy time in Europe for a major consolidation of air power there and in the Middle East. It was assumed now that atomic weapons would be used from the outset and that these and conventional forces would conduct integrated operations but now with a clear emphasis on destroying the Soviet war machine.

Much hinged on the air campaign and while these war plans involved land, sea and air forces, the initial blows were assumed to fall under the remit of the United States Air Force and its Strategic Air Command. The Air Force was quite open, if not explicit, in

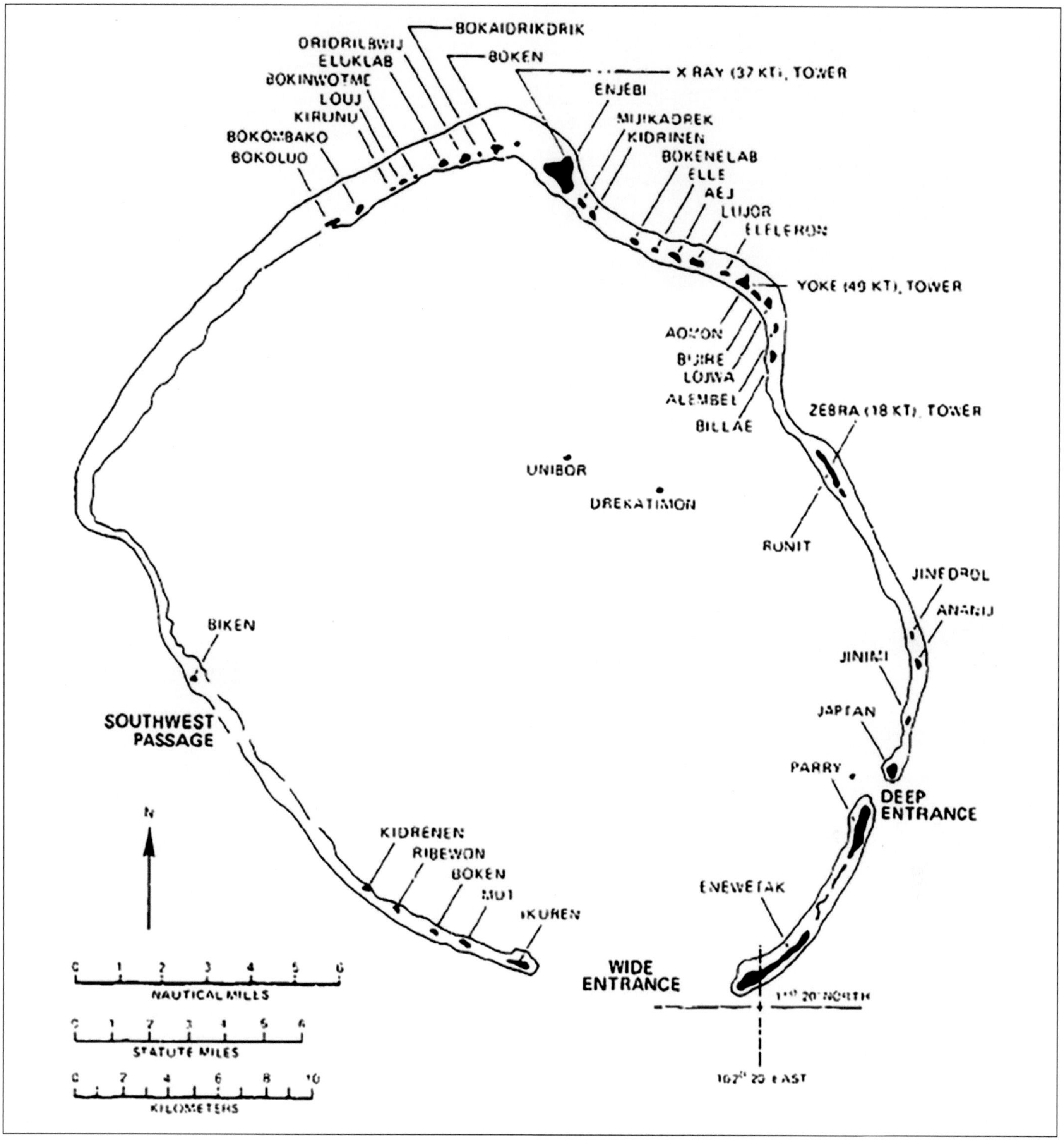

Eniwetok Atoll where the SANDSTONE atomic test was conducted by the Atomic Energy Commission, which sought to demonstrate technical progress with a refined bomb design rather than demonstrate effects as had been the purpose of the US Air Force Crossroad test in 1946. (AEC)

publicising these high-level requirements. In an article for *Collier's* magazine, Air Force Chief General Carl Spaatz defined for readers the true purpose of a future war, in that it was 'designed to destroy an enemy's home base and spare him nothing', that atom bombs would be used directly against the Red Army in a process of 'retardation' of ground forces as they surged across the German plains.

The size and scale of the initial air assault on Russia and Soviet forces was far larger than proposed in earlier war plans, with the first in a four-phase attack targeting 26 centres of manufacturing and industrial weapons production with 220 bombs on 104 urban centres. B-29 and B-50 bombers would reach their targets by means of mid-air refuelling using KB-29 tankers, as noted earlier. The delivery of atomic bombs would call for 300 bombers covering 6,000 sorties in the initial phase. The B-50s were assigned to hit 51 percent of targets, the B-29s hitting 35 percent, the remaining 14 percent addressed by the new B-36. The atomic attacks were to be concentrated in the opening days with the majority of all missions completed in 30 days. The B-29s and B-50s would fly out of the UK and this initial phase would last three months with heavy concentration of electronic countermeasures.

But there were severe critics of OFFTACKLE and the newly formed Weapons System Evaluation Group (WSEG), which had been formed on 11 December 1948 and notified to the press on 7 January 1949, took a detailed look at the plan and compared that

Significant consolidation of allied agreements on defence coalition saw the establishment of the North Atlantic Treaty Organisation (NATO) when President Truman (seated) and Secretary of State Acheson (holding books) signed the Instrument of Accession on 25 July 1949. (The White House)

with capabilities declared plausible from the various Command structures essential for its prosecution. The WSEG was set up to conduct analytical examination of weapon applications and the independent studies on warfighting potential at either an equipment or Command level so as to provide the Department of Defense with an apolitical judgement on claims made. It would remain effective until disbanded in 1976.

At the suggestion of Dr Vannevar Bush, the WSEG was founded by Secretary of Defense James Forrestal 'to provide rigorous, unprejudiced and independent analysis of evolutions of present and future weapons systems under probable future combat conditions – prepared by the ablest professional minds, military and civilians, and the most advanced analytical methods that can be brought to bear'. Located in the Pentagon not far from the offices of the JCS, in its initial adjudications on war plans presented by OFFTACKLE, it was a thorn in the side of the Air Force and a challenge to SAC because it exposed assumptions beyond capabilities. The WSEG was a small organisation, by mid-1949 only 35 staffers but it had access to a wide range of sources.

Scrutiny

Analysis of OFFTACKLE arrived at WSEG's desk by way of a question arising from briefings made to Truman by the Department of Defense on 20 April 1949 about SAC bombing plans. The President wanted a more detailed answer regarding the ability of US bombers to effectively reach their targets and what the effect of those raids might be. By this date Johnson had replaced Forrestal as Secretary of Defense and advised Truman that the JCS would respond and on 3 May the President was informed that this would be completed by the WSEG. At this time the Navy was still waging a funding war against the B-36, claiming that the Russians would shoot it down before it reached its target and the answer had bigger implications than that posed by the question.

For some time there was a suggestion that the WSEG would be well placed to make a final and conclusive judgement over the contested weapon systems regarding the B-36 or a naval carrier force for strategic delivery of atomic weapons but it was wisely judged that this decision was just as much a political judgement as it was technical, even a strategic one. But OFFTACKLE was well within the remit of the WSEG and that was to be one of its earliest deliberations.

On examining the war plan, a 22-man team at WSEG found that the number of sorties required in the opening phase was three times that available to SAC, at most 2,000 of the 6,000 required and that it could conduct 1,500–2,000 sorties for the first two months only if there was no other demand on the air transport inventory. The

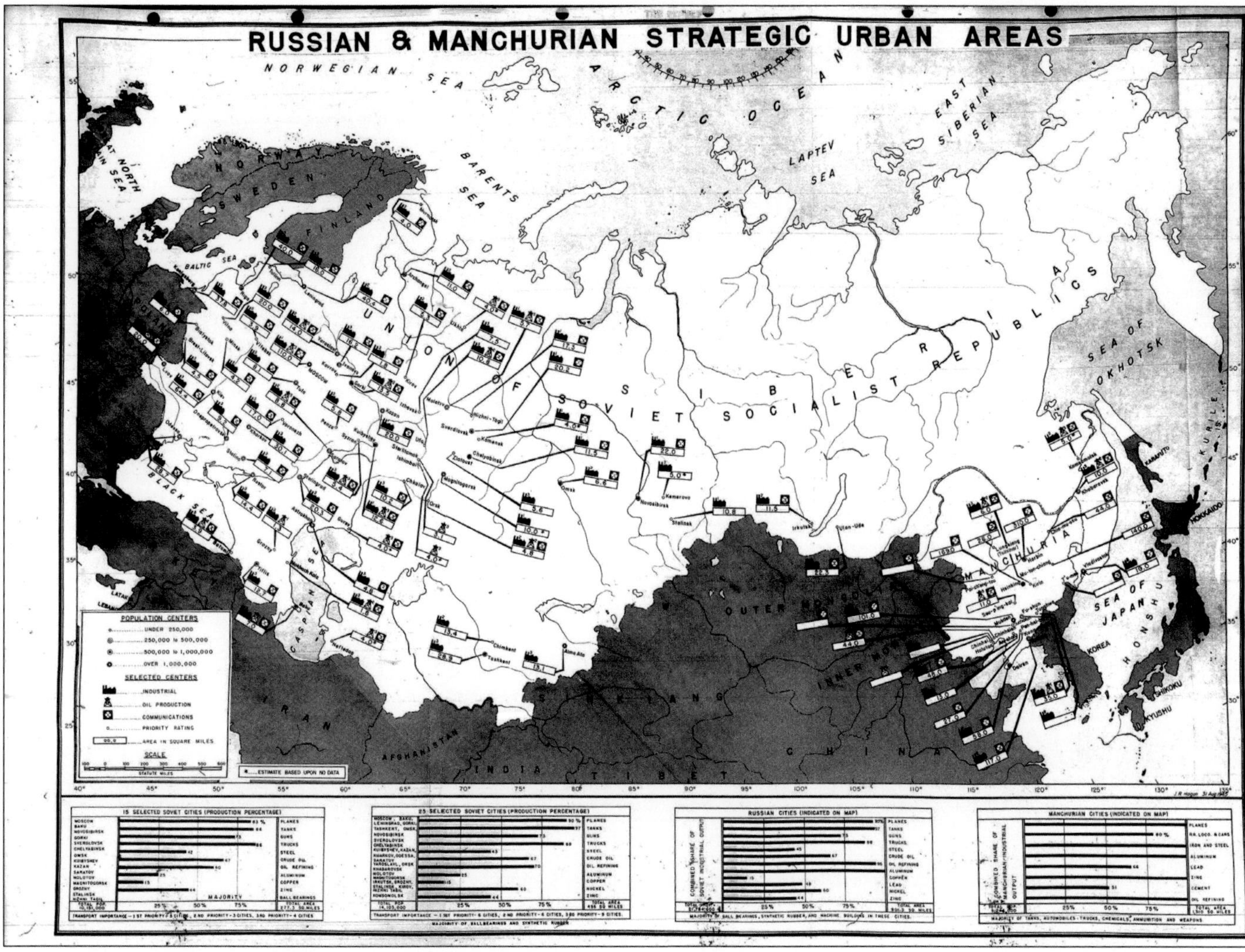

A consolidation of Soviet and Manchurian strategic resources and industrial assets, as assembled by the Air Force for OFFTACKLE, a war fighting plan involving massive atomic attack. (USAF)

SAC estimate for MATS transport availability, which was core to the plan, required 360 sorties by C-54s in the first few weeks but WSEG found that only 260 sorties could be made available to SAC. Given the priority placed by Eisenhower on consolidating operations from the UK and Europe, there would be heavy demands on transport aircraft for that alone.

There were concerns too about the number of aircraft available to conduct the required missions. The B-29s and B-50s would be expected to conduct missions other than supporting fully strategic operations and SAC had assumed that 1,800 B-29s could be brought out of storage but the actual stored inventory was running down, a factor which had been disregarded for OFFTACKLE. Moreover, contraction of the entire supporting infrastructure due to defence cuts reduced the quantity of 100/130-grade gasoline below the level required to support the plan and the emergency war reserve was below the required level too. It also found that forward basing of medium bombers was compromised by inadequate facilities in England with some airfields deficient in essential equipment. Neither was there adequate air defence for these airfields, the possibility of Soviet air attacks potentially rendering them useless.

The WSEG also discovered that the targets selected for both medium and heavy bombers which would fly from these assumed forward bases were problematic, in that there was no intelligence for half the 123 targets defined as priority for the first phase of an atomic attack. With only one reconnaissance wing available of the four deemed necessary for verifying targets, SAC was abysmally short on the necessary equipment as well as trained crewmembers required to fly reconnaissance flights and assemble target folders for the bombers. Without effective target information the folders would be empty until put together during the period the initial phase was under way. Most intelligence information on Russian targets came from scavenged Luftwaffe photographic files obtained before and during the Wehrmacht attack on Russia in 1941 but they were fragmentary at best.

There was additional concern over the paucity of electronic countermeasures due to a lack of equipment, trained personnel, chaff and associated dispensers and uncertainty as to how effective Russian forces were at countering intruders using ground radar. Vulnerability was a key 'unknown', along with uncertainties regarding Soviet air defences linked to fighters defending value-targets. SAC was depleted in escort fighters and the Republic F-84 that was planned for this task had yet to receive long-range tanks, a deficiency reminiscent of the situation over Europe in 1942 and 1943 until the P-51 could escort the B-17s and B-24s all the way out and back. There had been no update on the capabilities of the Soviet PVO beyond the expectation that they could field approximately 1,600 fighters.

Assessment of the balance in different munitions showed that the atomic bombing mission would only succeed if it was the exclusive priority for the initial phase and that conventional bombing assigned to drop 17,000 tons (15,422 tonnes) in 3,522 sorties could not be accomplished under those circumstances. The WSEG

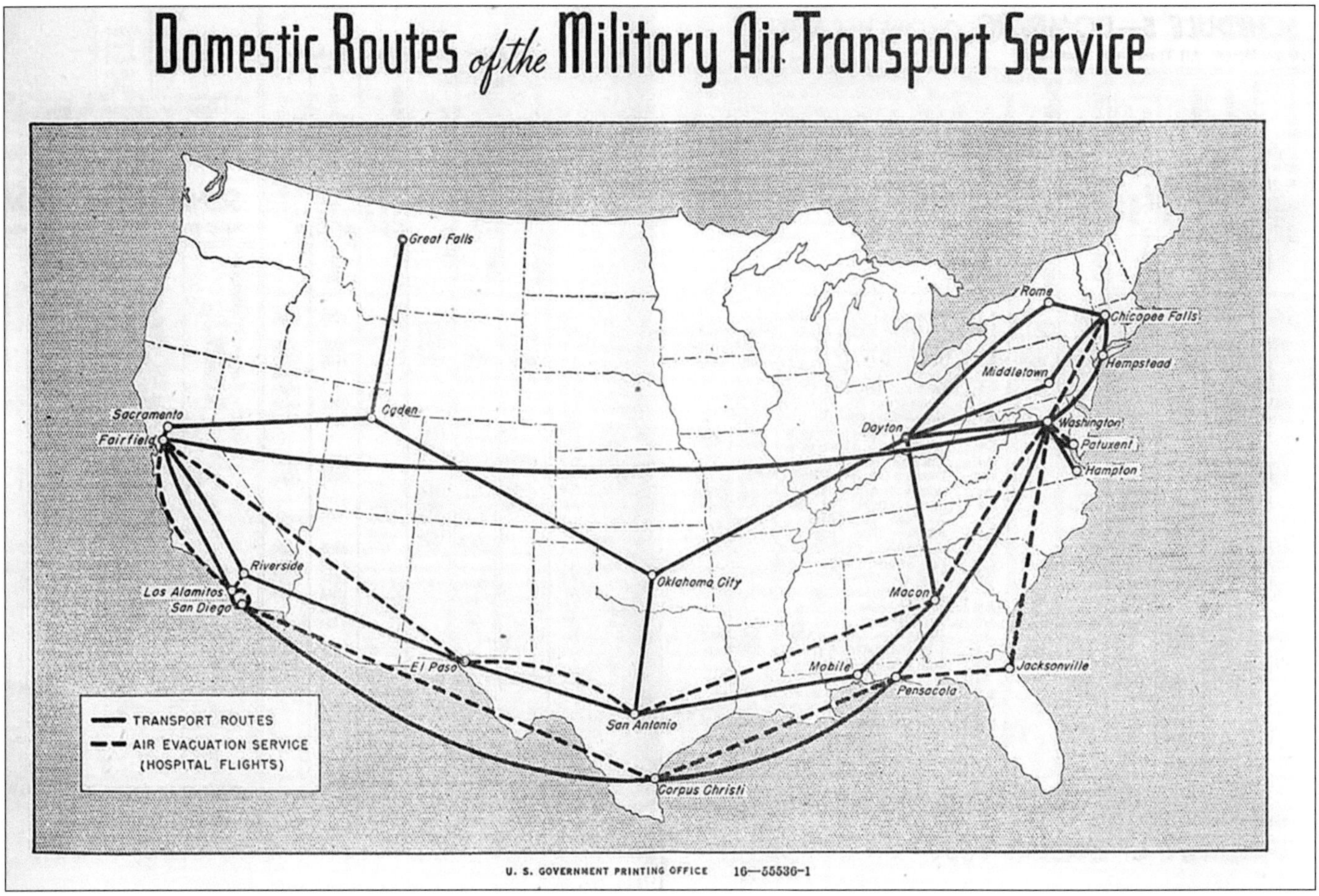

MATS provided a continental support net of scheduled routes for supplying air bases and replenishing combat units. (USAF)

noted that the atomic attack alone would account for a third of all weight carried by SAC. Nevertheless, despite the delivery of B-36 aircraft, it was evident that SAC would have been stressed beyond previously demonstrated levels to accomplish the overall objective of OFFTACKLE had war broken out at the end of 1949. Despite reservations, the war plan was accepted on 8 February 1950. It is perhaps ironic that this was based to some considerable degree by the observation that enough 'planning time has already been spent on the current emergency plan, to the detriment of mobilisation planning, intermediate range planning, and next year's emergency planning' and thus it would remain standard for at least the next two years.

While the WSEG addressed the needs of the Pentagon for a wide and objective examination of the plan, even before OFFTACKLE the Air Force was asked by the JCS to stand back and evaluate the realistic value of atomic bombing and examine the probability that it would achieve the claimed objective. The task was given to a six-member committee chaired by Air Force General Hubert Harmon, which began work in January 1949 based largely on TROJAN. It looked at the 70 primary targets and assessed that with both conventional and atomic bombing, 30–40 percent of Soviet industrial capacity would be 'reduced' but that this would not be permanent and recuperation would depend upon bounce-back time and priority organised by the State authorities.

When evaluating consequences, the Harmon study found that the most enduring damage would be caused by attacks on the petrochemical and petroleum industries. The damage to housing and infrastructure from attacks on cities and urban centres would yield an estimated 2.7 million Soviet dead and an additional four million casualties with life on the brink for a further 28 million. The general conclusion held to the notion that far from causing a breakdown in Soviet society, these figures would inure in the population a resolve previously seen in German blitz raids on England, combined Allied bombing raids on Germany and on the Russian population by the German attacks on their homeland.

Disturbingly, Harmon concluded that Soviet fighting capabilities would remain in the Middle East and into Western Europe but found that here too the resilience in the fuel supply chain would be directly proportional to erosion of supply caused by air power. Furthermore, it believed that a significant danger would exist should the Russians be driven to the point where their national survival was threatened, tipping them into an all-out reciprocal response with their own atomic weapons in an attempt to bring down their opponent. Perhaps surprisingly, given the exclusively military nature of the Harmon committee, it was concerned that while the use of atomic weapons could achieve unprecedented results, the military benefits could readily be overwhelmed by 'certain psychological and retaliatory reactions detrimental to the achievement of Allied war objectives'.

This was the first time an all-military committee had raised serious concerns about the potentially counterproductive use of atomic weapons in wartime, indicating concern for the broader range of strategic and political goals and objectives. Along with the WSEG report, Harmon provided a sober conclusion that stimulated debate at the Pentagon but did little to dissuade the Air Force and only endorse the resolve of SAC to deliver unconstrained force upon an enemy. The Army and the Navy discussed the consequences for

MATS routes for international deliveries supported all major areas of need, with routine supply networks together with occasional 'on-demand' requirements. (USAF)

their own war strategies in an environment in which it seemed that the Air Force assumed the leading role and the other services were reduced to supporting roles.

A comprehensive and unselective bombing plan was fundamental to what SAC referred to as its 'city-busting' plan, invoking the attitude of the Second World War by employing a 'horizontal target system' in which 'we didn't care if we were shooting at churches, industry, government centers, we (just) wanted to level the town', as quoted in the US Strategic Bombing Campaign Summary Report (European War) of 30 September 1945, page 16. But there were deep concerns that the Air Force was over-optimistic and that SAC was in danger of a self-imposed hubris, deluded into a self-belief of unimpeded waves of destruction bringing a 'rain (of destruction) from the skies'.

In evaluating the type and number of targets there had been no discrimination or collateral analysis of how specific sites could be integrated within the total spectrum of warfighting. Given the limited quantities of atomic bombs available, some uniformed observers worried that SAC could easily run out of munitions before resorting to conventional bombing to finish the task, which in itself would require considerably greater numbers of aircraft than would be available. Gone were the principles of targeted bombing and pinpoint selection of specific military or industrial targets in urban areas, replaced by the belief in systematic destruction of the entire district to take out the critical facilities. There was also a dire absence of accurate data on the effects of atomic bombs. With control firmly in the hands of the AEC, an unwillingness to share atomic weapons-effects results left planners for these war strategies using information extrapolated from bomb damage assessments in the Second World War.

The WSEG also noted the inadequate level of intelligence and looked closely at SAC plans for getting better information with which to plan attacks. The RB-29s were considered vulnerable and doubts were expressed about their survivability, the RB-36 only becoming available at the end of 1949 and then leaving much to be desired regarding operability and equipment, much of which was still in development along with the aircraft itself. With a crew of up to 22 and a complex array of sensory equipment and cameras, it would be some time before the RB-36 became fully operational and, while the RB-47 promised much, that type was still some time away from being available.

Inadequacies

Survival was key to mission success. What was known about Soviet air defence plans gave grim answers to questions about survivability. In 1948 the PVO had gained independence from the Directorate of Artillery and made significant improvements to ground-based anti-aircraft artillery (AAA), which had effectively been developed in response to higher operating altitudes for US aircraft. At the end of the Second World War Russian 85mm artillery could knock down aircraft at up to 37,000ft (11,277m) and very soon after the B-36 entered service, 100mm cannon were introduced, effective at up to 49,000ft (14,935m), higher than the bomb-laden intruder could reach. Much later, in the age of the all-jet bomber force, the Russians fielded 130mm guns effective to 70,000ft (21,336m). Added to which were the high-flying MiG jet-fighters armed with 23mm cannon and 37mm guns.

Integrating Russian air defence elements as known in 1949, the WSEG assessed the survival of a daylight attack force consisting of 223 B-29s and B-50s carrying 32 atom bombs, concluding that 35 aircraft would be shot down by enemy fighters, two to AAA, five due to technical issues and 14 turning back for various reasons. In all, 24 atom bomb-carriers would reach their assigned targets, three would be shot down, five lost for operational reasons and three completely missing their targets. This produced an aircraft loss rate of 19 percent and an ordnance delivery rate of 75 percent on target. The projected loss ratio was twice the average experienced by the Eighth AF in the Second World War.

For night raids, assuming 96 B-29s and B-50s carrying 32 atom bombs, seven would be shot down by fighters, two brought down by AAA and two to operational failures. Three bombs would fail to get delivered as planned, four aircraft would be lost due to technical issues and two bombs would miss their planned targets. In this case, losses would be 12 percent with a 92 percent bomb-dropping success. But in both cases the loss rates would be totally unacceptable and the attrition rate so high that none of the overall objectives could have been met. SAC would have run out of aircraft, crews and an ability to sustain the offensive.

LeMay was dismissive of these conclusions, citing an inflated interpretation of how numerous and effective the Soviet air defences were and asserting that 'We didn't have to worry about winning the air power battle because the Russians have no threat against us… we could ignore the rule book in winning the air power battle and go about destroying their resources'. Aside from confidence and an over-exerted tendency to simplify the challenge and project an overconfident belief in the prevalence of American air power projection, some could say that LeMay was himself looking to fight the next war with the methods of the last one, because all his statements are clear summations of what he faced against Imperial Japan and how he operated the B-29s to wreak havoc on its cities, unimpeded by the constraints of effective air defences.

Of all the various war plans put together between 1945 and 1950, OFFTACKLE was arguably the least effective, because it assumed a predominant role for the atomic bomb and was largely independent of strategies assembled by the Army and by the Navy. All three prime armed services were guilty of placing their own forces at the centre of military objectives and OFFTACKLE failed most because it was the first to incorporate a political objective, one which would not attempt to completely topple the state but to totally supress Russia's ability to wage war. To do that it required a truly unified approach to the objectives and it failed that test at almost every level.

Equally impressive and comprehensive war plans and strategies had been put together by the Army and the Navy and had been notionally integrated into Air Force projections in the plans described above. But the mistaken idea that the Air Force and its strategic bomber force could win a future war had dominated thinking to the exclusion of land and naval forces, which would have been essential to holding Western Europe and the Middle East. Almost single-mindedly, SAC and cost-effective atomic air power dominated the newly independent Air Force, perhaps a hubristic elevation of expectation arising from that alone. But, as noted at the top of this book, politicians were only too keen to accept that promise for all the defence dollars it saved.

It was for this reason that Congress had funded development of the B-36, the B-47 and early studies into a long-range successor to the B-36, eventually designated B-52. But for the period 1945–1949, the B-29 and the B-50 formed the mainstay of war plans and operational effectiveness. Under the revised designation of type classification, in early 1950 SAC had 512 bombers including 337 B-29s and 148 B-50 medium and 27 B-36 heavy bombers. The core aircraft was itself a relative newcomer, the B-29 having only begun to build its reputation when it made its first operational bombing raid on Japan in June 1944, the last aircraft being delivered in May 1946, another victim to post-war contraction and massive defence budget cuts.

Development of the B-29 had been a long and painful process with frequent threats to cancel it as technical and engineering challenges almost brought it down. Yet it became the iconic symbol of American air power and was deployed on publicity campaigns after the war as the weapon that defeated Japan and dropped the bomb that the Air Force claimed, true or not, had forced Japan to surrender. When introduced, the B-29 was the most advanced bomber in service anywhere and despite being one of the most complex aircraft built, it bristled with technological innovations and advanced design features.

Oversold at birth as the 'Hemispheric Defense Weapon', the B-29 had self-sealing fuel tanks, pressurised crew compartments, remotely controlled heavy air defence armament, a maximum bomb load of 20,000lb (9,072kg) over short distances and a maximum range of 3,250 miles (5,229km) and a service ceiling of 31,859ft (9,708m). It was powered by four R-3350 turbocharged engines producing 2,200hp (1,640kw) and built by the Curtis-Wright Corporation. But they had serious problems, the engines frequently overheating, blowing cylinder heads off on starting up, suffering from faulty ignition circuits, leaking oil and poor fuel systems. Under operational conditions, engines had a life of only 270 flying hours before replacement.

A victim of 'concurrency', where aircraft enter production nursing teething troubles, the B-29 had many problems from the outset. The engine required more than 2,000 modifications and changes, with each aircraft initially deployed with a spare engine in a bomb bay. Rushing to get the aircraft into service and begin operations against mainland Japan, the AAF struggled to keep enough aircraft available but with intense effort the B-29 emerged as a war-winning tool for strategic bombing, but not without compromise. Poor engine performance and troubles at altitude were some reasons why LeMay brought the bombers down low to attack Japanese cities. After the war, modifications and problems were still being corrected when the B-29 went out of service in 1953 leaving only a few KB-29 tankers to soldier on.

Never designed for anything other than conventional bombs, the B-29 required considerable rework to make them capable of carrying atom bombs under a programme known as SILVERPLATE. These changes and modifications were introduced according to when

Atmospheric response to an atomic detonation would dictate the proximity of aircraft and in weapons testing this became one critical measurement from patrolling air-samplers. (Department of Energy)

specific aircraft came through the production cycle and were mostly associated with changes to the bomb bay. For these purposes the B-29 was equipped with the slightly improved R-3350-41 engine which had improved cooling, fuel-injection and an upgraded manifold system. The remotely controlled gun turrets were removed but the tail guns were retained and the aircraft were equipped with reverse-pitch propellers to assist with braking after landing. Some of these changes were made at base rather than before delivery.

Initially, most adaptations included pneumatic bomb bay doors, replacing the standard electrically driven ones. This allowed the aircraft to get cleaned up as quickly as possible after dropping its atom bomb to give it better performance while conducting a 155-degree diving turn at 60-degree bank angle, losing 1,700ft (518m) immediately after bomb release. In this way the aircraft would be 10 miles (16km) away at the point of detonation, increasing the safety margin by a factor of two. The blast effect data had been obtained through theoretical calculations and over time by measurements during CROSSROADS and SANDSTONE tests.

As noted earlier, the Mk III was to be the first production bomb carried by the B-29. With plutonium as the core it was the operational version of 'Fat Man' and was effectively a live weapon from the time it was assembled, requiring an initiator (the 'urchin') and a shell, all three components being referred to as the 'pit'. With the high explosive detonators in place the bomb was armed and made live with electrical circuits for high voltage power source to sequence the release, fusing and detonation of the explosives which would initiate the chain reaction. Safety devices, electrical circuits and plugs ensured the bomb would not detonate prematurely.

The detonators had a shelf life of nine days and that effectively gave the weapon its stored duration and the batteries had to be recharged every 36 hours and cleaned every nine days. Because of thermal heating in the core, it could be left in place for only 10 days to ensure it would not damage the initiators. Several modifications and improvements were made to the refined Mk IV bomb which had an integrated uranium and plutonium pit and further improvements later on allowed interchangeability of these components to selectively change the yield of the bomb so that it could be 'shaped' for specific targets. As noted previously, it was this development which was tested during SANDSTONE.

The pit was installed before flight or sometimes during flight facilitated by doors in the nose of the bomb and a port through the casing to allow access to the pit, which was coated in metals to shield the crew from radiation. Any corrosion would leak radiation harmful to the crew. Changes to the way the detonators were configured offered some safety in preventing unexpected detonation in the event the carrier-plane crashed. Operations with the Mk IV were considerably safer than with the Mk III and ease of use and installation was a great improvement, preventing inadmissible procedures and enhancing fail-safe handling.

SILVERPLATE called for 65 B-29s to be capable of carrying the atom bomb and at the time of the Japanese surrender, 46 aircraft had been so modified, of which 26 were available for operational use for tests at Sandia Laboratories or at Wendover Field, Utah, and 17 were placed in storage. Orders were issued by Air Materiel Command (AMC) on 26 July 1946 for the additional 19 to be modified to SILVERPLATE standard but deterioration of airframes reduced the number of aircraft operational, only 18 being available to SAC by 1 October 1947. Due to a security scare the name for the conversion programme was changed to SADDLETREE on 12 May 1947 and aircraft embraced by the modifications now included the B-29, B-50A and the B-36.

Modifications for the B-50A included a new bomb rack with special attachment points. The structure was known as the Auxiliary Bomb Rack, or the Universal Suspension and Release System (U-1) so as to veil the true purpose of the device. It consisted of vertical support rails that would connect with the existing supports for conventional bombs. This held a horizontal structure which when fitted resembled an H, so it became known as the H-frame, capable of carrying a 'Fat Man' or a 'Little Boy' bomb together with electrical monitoring and control equipment with readouts and controls from a panel in the forward pressurised compartment. With four sway braces in place, the bomb was connected to electrical lines for safeing and arming, access being provided by walkways to allow the weaponeer to arm the Mk III or insert the pit for the Mk IV.

Like the B-29, the B-50A had not been developed for atomic bombs but as introduced it was capable of carrying either a single atom bomb or up to 20,000lb (9,072kg) of conventional ordnance with flights ranging over the North Pole. Flights from Alaska or England would be range-limited for a direct return to base and options were to either divert to other airfields or accept the inevitability of a one-way flight. Rarely discussed, the grim prospect of a one-way flight was accepted without question and the topic is only infrequently mentioned in official documents and completely lacking in rehearsals and simulated attacks where return flight paths are found to be absent.

Because of the lack of information about detailed design, precise dimensions and handling criteria for the Mk III and Mk IV atom bombs, Boeing was unable to deliver B-50As equipped for carrying them and all modifications had to go through the SADDLETREE programme, including the provision of special equipment for the weaponeer, as noted above. But the aircraft had to be adaptable, the low numbers of atom bombs held for use required the aircraft to be capable of also flying conventional missions. For that reason, the Auxiliary Bomb Rack could be changed out in 24 hours, restoring the aircraft to a conventional bomber. SADDLETREE modifications for 69 B-50As began in April 1948 and by 31 March 1949 the conversions had been completed.

4
STRATEGIC AIR COMMAND

After XX Bomber Command began operations against the Japanese mainland in August 1944 and XXI Bomber Command from the Marianas, the B-29 played a truly decisive role in ending the Second World War. Before the two atomic raids on Hiroshima and Nagasaki, 91 percent of all bombs dropped on Japan had been carried to their targets by this aircraft, burning out 66 percent of all urban areas and virtually halting any meaningful continuation of the war. It is no overstatement to say that the performance of this aircraft in that war did much to instil in the armed services that strategic air power would be crucial to success in future wars and that, for the time being at least, the B-29 would be a critical national asset.

Long before the AAF entered the peacetime era and prepared for defence consolidation and independence as the United States Air Force, senior leaders contemplated the way the future force would be organised. With the assumption that the strategic bombing capabilities already in place would be the cornerstone of future forces, it was a natural path for reconfiguration from the conventional to the atomic era in air warfare planning. A new structure would be needed for the atomic age and for the jet age which together would usher in a very different and much more sobering capability.

Shortly after the dropping of the second atomic bomb on Nagasaki, Major General Curtis LeMay moved to begin a process of raising the issue to top priority. The war was clearly over and as Chief of Staff for the US Army Strategic Air Forces in the Pacific, LeMay played a key role in orchestrating such a discussion, which he did on 30 August 1945 in a message to General Ira Eaker, Deputy Commander of the AAF. LeMay wanted the 509th Bomb Group responsible for dropping the atomic bombs on Japan to be the nucleus of a new, peacetime command carrying the strategic nuclear deterrent. Clearly, this was going to be LeMay's show.

Eaker responded by requesting generals Carl Spaatz, Hoyt Vandenberg and Lauris Norstad to assemble a body of specialist officers to put together an organisational structure and assess requirements. They met between 18 September and 23 October and submitted recommendations to General Arnold. It was already clear that atomic bombs would be extremely expensive and probably only available in relatively small numbers and they concluded that the atomic bomb was best deployed within a mix of conventional ordnance and used sparingly.

Prescient to the report presented two years later after Operation SANDSTONE and before full analysis of the Hiroshima and Nagasaki raids, it believed the atomic bomb would be most effectively used against 'large urban and industrial targets'. It was less enamoured with the atom bomb as a 'silver bullet' capable of ending conflict at a stroke, seeing it as one additional arrow in the quiver rather than the panacea for all strategic challenges that the press had hailed the new weapon to be. Very few people truly understood the science behind 'the bomb', least of all the press, and public attitudes had already begun to gather around both pragmatic and moral opinion. General Arnold threw his weight behind the group's recommendations and installed LeMay as Deputy Chief of Staff for Research and Development, adding career clusters to his stars.

LeMay was a natural choice, both credible and capable and brought a high level of experience. After commanding the 305th BG in England between October 1942 and May 1943, he commanded the freshly minted 3rd Air Division and personally led many dangerous missions including the Schweinfurt-Regensburg raid on 17 August 1943 in which 24 aircraft were shot down. Always insisting on being in the lead bomber and defined by some as a 'brutal' commander, at a time when many crews were aborting back to base LeMay insisted that the entire crew of any aircraft that turned back before reaching its target would be court-martialled. The number of aborted flights went down dramatically. In August 1944 LeMay was assigned to the XX Bomber Command in China and from there to XXI Bomber Command in the Pacific.

Successful in devising techniques to improve the efficiency of combat formations in Europe, he redefined the way the B-29s operated by shifting from daylight, high-altitude runs to night-time, low-altitude flight paths, thus avoiding defensive fighters. In a major campaign between March and August 1945, LeMay presided over the destruction of large swaths of the Japanese industrial base, burning out numerous cities, exacting a great toll in human life and probably doing at least as much as the two atom bombs to bring the country to its knees and pulling forward the day of its surrender. LeMay had always interpreted his job as shortening the war and he believed that in achieving what he had done that task had been accomplished.

Criticised by some for a belligerent, uncompromising approach to command, the commitment and resolve that LeMay unquestionably brought to all his assignments made him a natural choice to head up the post-war strategic bombing force. He was a bomber pilot to the core and took great pains to ensure his men received the best the government could provide, often in times of fiscal restraint where resources were scarce and residential quarters on or off the base were parlous at best. In that, he received recognition and loyalty, introducing several beneficial approaches that increased the effectiveness of the units under his command and the efficiency of the crews.

Under the authority placed on him by General Arnold, LeMay would collect all the various strands of the AAF's research and development programmes but also act as liaison between the Air Staff and the Manhattan Engineering District, the Army headquarters for the Manhattan Project being in that part of New York city. Concurrent with this action, the Air Staff began planning for an Atomic Bomb Striking Force (ABSF) but Eaker objected to that name as it might imply that this component of the total bomber force was all that was necessary as 'the only strategic air force that we will require', insisting that the word 'Atomic' be deleted.

In March 1946 the reorganisation of the AAF retired the Continental Air Forces (CAF), which had only been in existence since 15 December 1944 to relieve the Air Staff of operational duties in the United States and allow more time for policy decisions. The first units for CAF were assigned on 16 April 1945 and it commanded operational control of them from 10 May 1945. In March 1946 three new commands were set up, of which one was Strategic Air Command (SAC), the other two being Air Defense Command (ADC) and Tactical Air Command (TAC). Headquarters First Air Force and Headquarters Fourth Air Force went to ADC at Mitchell Field, New York. Headquarters Third Air Force and Headquarters IX Troop Command were moved to TAC at Tampa, Florida. SAC received Headquarters Second Air Force and would remain in existence throughout the Cold War. TAC and ADC would be deactivated on 1 December 1948 and reactivated on 1 December 1950 and 1 January 1951, respectively.

CAF had wide and somewhat diverse responsibilities, carrying out all functions within the Zone of the Interior insofar as unit movements between European and the Pacific theatres were concerned and after the end of the war it would play a significant role in administering demobilisation in the United States as servicemen returned or were discharged from home bases. It had also been responsible for national air defence, training and forming up a Continental Strategic Reserve. As such its success could be measured by the rapidity with which it put itself out of business.

SAC officially came into existence on 12 March 1946 with a clear mandate to deliver a strategic response to unprovoked aggression and to integrate the deployment of both conventional and atomic weapons, although at its formation the precise model for how they would be utilised had yet to be decided. Headquarters Second AF was deactivated on 30 March 1946 and Headquarters Fifteenth AF was assigned to SAC, effective 31 March from Colorado Springs,

B-29s of the 462nd BG, XX Bomber Command at West Field on Tinian in the Marianas Islands from where a major series of raids was mounted by the US Air Force. (USAF)

Hosting B-29s of the 29th BG at North Field, Guam. Guam was taken by the Japanese on 8 December 1941 and retaken by the Americans on 21 July 1944. (USAF)

With the abiding motto 'Peace is Our Profession', Strategic Air Command forged a new identity from historic achievements in US AAF groups during the Second World War creating the most feared but revered instrument for retribution in the aftermath of an unprovoked attack. (USAF-SAC)

Colorado, absorbing all its personnel and equipment. As noted previously, the SAC mission had been defined some time before it was established but the formal mission was expressed by General Spaatz as follows:

> The Strategic Air Command will be prepared to conduct long range offensive operations in any part of the world either independently or in cooperation with land and Naval forces; to conduct maximum range reconnaissance over land or sea either independently or in cooperation with Naval forces; to provide combat units capable of intense and sustained combat operations employing the latest and most advanced weapons; to train units and personnel for the maintenance of the Strategic Forces in all parts of the world; to perform such special missions as the Commanding General, Army Air Forces may direct.

At the end of March 1946, SAC had 55 airfields and installations and 43 of those went to the Fifteenth AF, most of which had been left over from wartime use. As the only operational command in SAC, the Fifteenth had the strategic B-29s but they were in varying states of readiness with no ability to operate effectively in a combat situation for several weeks. General George C Kenney was given command of SAC, a position which he served from 21 March 1946 to 19 October 1948. Brigadier General Charles F Born was in command of Fifteenth AF until 15 April 1947. Three important units were VIII Bomber Command (VH) at Peterson Field, Colorado Springs, the 58th Very Heavy Bombardment Wing assigned atomic bomb duties and the 73rd Very Heavy Bombardment Wing at MacDill Army Air Field, Florida. Below wing level came the 509th Composite Group at Roswell Army Air Base, New Mexico, the 58th Very Heavy Bombardment Wing and the 12 Very Heavy Bombardment Groups assigned to SAC from the outset.

The 311th Reconnaissance Wing was assigned to Fifteenth AF from 1 August and the Eighth AF was operating under Headquarters Fifteenth AF and moved from MacDill to Fort Worth Army Air Field on 1 November. VIII Bomber Command had been tasked with Operation Wonderful, the administrative management of six very heavy bomber and tactical and service units of the Second AF assigned to overseas duty. This came to an end on 10 November due to administrative objections from overseas commanders.

The fighter forces assigned to SAC fluctuated greatly in purpose and strength as the definition of the role within that command

Built by Bell, this B-29B of the 315th BW (44-84061) named *Pacusan Dreamboat* was delivered on 20 July 1945, upgraded with R-3350-79 fuel-injection engines and re-designated YB-29J. It made a number of record-breaking flights. (USAF)

changed with evolving bomber capabilities. As a legacy of the Second World War, initially the fighter was viewed as an escort for the bombers and the assignment of units to SAC can be found in *Volume 1: Fighters 1945–1949* but manning of the two groups on hand by September 1946 (56th FG and 4th FG) did not begin until March 1947, in which year three new groups (27th FG, 33rd FG and 82nd FG) were activated with SAC. The five groups were reassigned as Wings from 1 August 1948 but by the end of that year three were reassigned to Continental Air Command followed by a fourth in mid-1949, at which date only one (27th) was retained in SAC and that was re-designated a Fighter Escort Wing on 1 February 1950.

At first, SAC fighter units were equipped with the P-51 and from 1947 by the P-80 in two of the groups followed by the F-84 in 1948 to supplement the twin-fuselage F-82 but SAC lost all its jets when three groups went to Continental Air Command (CAC) at the end of the year. Some F-86 aircraft with the 1st Fighter Wing served with SAC for a few months in 1949–50 but, with short range and optimised for interception, they were little use in the escort role.

As conversion from piston-engine to jet-engine types began to take hold across the Air Force, problems with the new and challenging technology created difficulties with servicing and maintenance. Conversion went through a difficult time in 1946 and 1947 and many lessons were learned about how to operate and best use the new types. The limited range of jet fighters in this period excluded them from bomber exercises and war planning, which increasingly came to support simulated, unescorted raids into enemy territory.

Berlin

On 9 August 1946 an American C-47 was shot down by Yugoslavian fighters while flying over that country, followed by another incident several hours later from ground fire bringing vigorous protest from the US Department of State. RAF Spitfires were sent up from the Klagenfurt area to try to find the second aircraft but without success. A flight of six B-29s from the 43rd BG at Davis-Monthan Field, Arizona led by Colonel James C Selser Jr, flew to Rhein-Main Airfield, Germany, in mid-November 1946.

Accompanied by two C-54s of the 1st Air Transport Unit out of Roswell Field, New Mexico, and with B-29s carrying spares and equipment, they remained there for two weeks and conducted several flights along Russian-occupied territory. They also visited airfields in Western Europe to judge their suitability for supporting the B-29 in the event of deployment there in what is regarded as the first use of the aircraft as an instrument of international diplomacy.

Only several months later, while SAC did not contribute directly to the Berlin airlift after the Russians imposed a blockade on the city, it played a vital role in projecting US willingness to stand up to Soviet aggression. Because it was the single instrument of strategic air capability, the B-29 played an important part. The airlift began on 25 June 1948 and would continue until 12 May 1949. Two days after it started, the US Air Force ordered SAC to build up its forces in Europe.

At that date, only one squadron of the 301st BG was in Germany, stationed at Fürstenfeldbruck on a rotation programme, and two more squadrons were moved up to Goose Bay, Labrador, prior to relocation to Germany. The 28th and 307th Very Heavy Bombardment Groups (VHBGs) were also placed on alert readiness for moving across the Atlantic Ocean on 12-hour and three-hour notice, respectively. The 301st had all three of its squadrons in Germany by the beginning of July while the 28th BG moved from Rapid City AFB, South Dakota, to RAF Scampton, England, and the 307th went from MacDill AFB, Florida, to RAF Marham and RAF Waddington, also in England.

A portent of future global requirements for an intercontinental air force, airfield construction in foreign fields during the Second World War brought experience which would be useful during the Cold War. (USAAF)

All deployments had been completed by 17 July and the alert status for the other groups was stood down. The deployments caused the squadrons to remain on standby, which prevented them from conducting training and familiarisation flights and that interfered with general operational exercises. The 301st was replaced by the 2nd BG which went to England but it returned to Europe to replace the 28th BG.

Deployments to England under Project LOOKER were the first since the Second World War and had been delayed somewhat by the need for procedures to be agreed with national and local authorities. Also because of essential arrangements in facilities and supporting equipment, as airfields that had not been expected to support American bombers, and certainly of a very different type to those which had frequented the country little more than three years previously, were appropriately configured.

Local reaction was largely an eruption of welcome re-connection with Britain's former colonials and many rural public houses remained open long after licensing hours feting the returnees, some of whom had been in England during the war and held strong connection with East Anglia. Interestingly, for the 28th's 30 aircraft operating out of RAF Marham, United States Air Forces Europe limited flight time to 7 hours for each aircraft per week, flight patterns remaining within UK airspace.

Deployed to the UK under Operation DAGGER, the 307th BG had previously been conducting antisubmarine training but with one squadron at Waddington and two at Scampton the opportunity was taken to carry out interception by RAF fighters against B-29s conducting a simulated attack on London during Battle of Britain Week, 13–19 September. The group returned to MacDill AFB on 2 November, replaced by the 22nd BG.

For the British, the period of the Berlin airlift had special poignancy. In contributing to the supply of grain for the German city, ships bound for Britain were redirected to German ports at the government's request and rationing was re-introduced, the first time that staple had been rationed in the UK, even in wartime. At US-occupied British bases, airmen again hosted parties for local children and quietly gave food to impoverished locals as they had during the American presence in England between 1942 and 1945.

The Berlin airlift had a profound significance for SAC too, jolted from a level of post-war complacency where war had previously seemed a remote possibility. A degree of apathy pervaded governments in West European countries, stoically gathering national and financial resources to restore a peacetime economy after several years of austerity or occupation. Quite suddenly, the severe military threat pervading events throughout the period of the Berlin blockade shook loose the nervous reticence not to host American military forces on their liberated land, now awakened to the new reality of a potential conflict, perhaps even attack and the use of atomic weapons not far beyond their borders.

Requests for US bases in West European countries tested diplomacy, as some countries feared the consequences of provoking a military response from the Soviet Union should they be seen as supporting mobilisation for war. In general, while they focused financial resources on restoring economic stability, governments were quite happy to have American taxpayers provide funds for the US Air Force to put up a shield against communist aggression, however reluctant many of the population across democratic European countries were to host foreign military units. Yet for all the checks and balances, SAC gained tremendous experience moving units across the Atlantic Ocean until it had honed a mobility programme which we will explore fully in *Volume 5: Bombers 1950–1953*.

The emergency deployments of 1948 were sustained throughout the period of tension to the point where the Russians backed down and the supply routes to Berlin from Western Europe opened once more. The reduction in force presence was gradual, ensuring that at least one full group remained in England from August 1949. But the requirement for a rapid mobilisation had a profound effect on planning for future, unforeseen eventualities and that became more important after the Russians detonated their first atomic bomb on 29 August 1949. In theory at least, there was now the impending threat of a nuclear war added to the political belligerence from Moscow and the uncertainties. This gave SAC the incentive through better funding and stronger support in Congress, whose members were increasingly concerned at increased tensions with Moscow.

Reflections and Change

As related earlier, the use of the B-29 as an instrument of diplomacy was crucial to the potential it implied by its presence. Moreover, as the key element in dropping one of the two atomic bombs tested at Bikini Atoll under Operation CROSSROADS on 1 July 1946, an activity which involved 42,000 men at sea, on land and in the air, it represented a poignant signal to Russia that it was continuing with development of the atomic bomb and was already characterising the effectiveness of the weapon.

In diplomatic circles, the immediate aftermath of the Second World War saw uncertainty as to how the atomic bomb would be regarded. Some American politicians sought international agreement on a universal ban on the possession of such weapons but it was a myopic vision sought by visionaries who had little grasp on how the Cold War was unfolding.

On establishment, in mid-1946 SAC had 279 tactical aircraft, of which 148 were B-29s and 85 were P-51s along with 31 F-2s and 15 C-54s. A year later it had a paper strength of 713 aircraft including 319 B-29s and 230 P-51s. Throughout 1947, SAC flew goodwill missions to England and several European countries as well as to South America. It also conducted a maximum-effort mission where several units flew simulated attacks on US cities, most notable being the 'attack' on New York on 16 May when it was deemed that 101 B-29s had successfully destroyed the city, although a further 30 could not participate as planned due to maintenance issues and lack of supplies.

As noted, 1948 was the first operational deployment of SAC aircraft in direct response to international tension and a potential military threat, when the B-29s were deployed in response to the Berlin blockade. In that year, SAC had 837 aircraft on strength, of which 486 were B-29s and 30 were RB-29 reconnaissance types, 35 were B-50s and 35 were B-36s. On 9 November, SAC Headquarters moved from Andrews AFB, Maryland, to Offutt AFB, Nebraska. It was a memorable year in which both the pace and the capability of SAC increased considerably with the inherent arrival of the first Boeing B-50A, on 20 February, and the Convair B-36A on 26 June.

These aircraft signalled a step change in both operations and war-planning potential, although the lack of atomic weapons still emphasised SAC's conventional bombing role. Previously, the B-29 had been categorised as a 'very heavy bomber' (VHB) but with the arrival of the much-improved B-50 and the massive B-36, this category was dropped and both B-29 and B-50 types were re-categorised as medium bombers while the B-36 was to be a heavy-bomber type, the word 'very' being dropped. New too was the role of tanker, as modified B-29s were re-categorised as KB-29Ms capable of inflight refuelling, the first of which had only basic modifications and utilised the British system of trailing hoses and grapple devices for connecting the aircraft together. The 43rd and 509th Air Refuelling Squadrons were activated at Davis-Monthan AFB on 18 June 1948.

By 1948 SAC was struggling with high levels of inefficiency and the teething troubles of a new range of aircraft including the all-jet B-45 Tornado, the six-engine B-36 and preparation for service introduction of the B-47 which, although still a few years away from service, heralded a vastly different era for the strategic role. All those aspects required planning for and conversion toward an all-jet force, which now included the future B-52 which in 1948 was being designed with jet engines supplanting the earlier proposals for turboprop engines. Above it all, General George Kenney was preoccupied with a range of responsibilities including being the US representative to the UN Military Staff Committee, a subsidiary to the UN Security Council advising it on operations and on armaments for the United States and partners.

Distracted by these and other service preoccupations, Kenney left most of the operational running of SAC to his deputy, Major General St Clair Streett who in January 1947 was replaced by Major General Clements McMullen. Morale suffered badly as a new training programme was introduced whereby crews were cross-trained in each other's jobs in a drive to reduce from five to three the number of officers on each aircraft. This created a poorly trained and orientated command structure with the level of effectiveness falling as a result, impacting operational readiness to the point SAC was ineffective in mission assignments and roles. Kenney was outspoken with public statements about the inevitability of a Soviet attack as soon as the communists acquired the atom bomb, attracting the ire of politicians asserting that serving officers had no role speculating on foreign policy.

Outspoken too about the teething troubles with the colossal B-36, his remarks were unhelpful when the Air Force was fighting for the programme against opposition in some Congressional circles. Believing that the B-36 was over-priced and short on delivery, Kenney proclaimed support for the B-50 instead, a completely redesigned B-29 but with more powerful engines. Burdens placed on

Logistics and support services from Military Air Transport Command was crucial to efficient use of the strategic bombing force but for SAC there were strategic support squadrons, some of which were equipped with the C-54, this example operated by MATS. (USAF)

A B-50D-75-80 (48-075) heads this line-up of like types operated by three squadrons of the 2nd BW at Hunter AFB, Georgia. (NARA)

A B-29B stands next to the XB-36 (42-13570) giving scale to the six-engine strategic bomber which would form the backbone of the heavy-bomber force from 1948. (Convair)

An ERB-45C (48-017) which was delivered to the Air Force on 15 August 1950 and modified to an electronic reconnaissance configuration. (USAF)

Formerly head of Far East Forces and from April 1946 chief of Strategic Air Command, General George Kenney brought a storied record of high achievement but failed to shape SAC into the organisation it would become after he was replaced by General Curtis LeMay in October 1948. (USAF)

Kenney outside his duty as commander of SAC brought doubt to the reputation of a man who, between 1942 and 1945, had transformed the flagging fortunes of the Fifth Air Force and honed it into a highly efficient force, as demonstrated by his use of B-25s imposing crushing defeat on the Japanese at the battle of the Bismarck Sea.

Yet for all that, there were fundamental reasons for Kenney's failure to hone SAC into an efficient fighting force. Supported by the globetrotting Kenney, McMullen stripped out non-flying officers and put the burden of desk jobs onto officers with qualified, flying experience but sowing frustration. McMullen was noted for his uncompromising demands, commenting once regarding subordinates that commanders should 'Give them half of what they ask for, work them twice as hard, and they will get twice as much done'. The effect was to demoralise and frustrate the natural tendency of an officer to first look after his men and then to harness and control resources for the management and prosecution of the assigned mission.

With clear and distinct inefficiencies and a flagging readiness for combat, General Spaatz admonished Kenney for these failures in leadership and delivery, while the new Chief of Staff, Hoyt Vandenberg, asked Charles Lindbergh to visit six SAC bases and provide his assessment of conditions and mission readiness. Spending more than 1,000 hours in the air with SAC crews, Lindbergh found low levels of morale, poor standards of professionalism, a lack of discipline, inadequate training and only a loose control over mandatory standards of maintenance and servicing. Moreover, crews were uncoordinated and lacking in solid teamwork, with a low level of integration and poor cross-familiarisation which had been a tenet of the Kenney/McMullen leadership.

Everywhere it seemed, on paper at least, SAC was shaping itself for the atomic age, with a new range of highly capable aircraft and a fighting force ready to man them just below the surface, however, things were very far from what they seemed to be. The 43rd and the 2nd BGs were assigned to be the next to get A-bomb-capable aircraft after the 509th. Already equipped with the B-29 and the B-50 while the B-36 would be coming in to squadrons. With the 2nd BG away in England it fell to the 43rd to begin to receive its first B-50s and the 7th BG at Carswell would too get the B-36B equipped for delivering the atomic bomb, replacing their initial tranche of less capable B-36As. Despite these moves, the large part of SAC would remain capable of delivering only conventional weapons. By September, half the six Groups in the Fifteenth AF were overseas, with two in England and one in Okinawa.

But there were disquieting reports of a Command in crisis. Much of the equipment carried by the B-29 was inherited from the Second World War and radar units were threatened by outdated components and many feared that they could be easily jammed by an enemy. SAC had 5,100 officers and 39,500 airmen with a paper strength of 420 aircraft but practice flights used targets with radar reflectors to virtually guarantee a lock despite the efficacy of the aircraft and its crew. Moreover, flight crews were reluctant to take their aircraft above 15,000ft (4,572m) to prevent icing or over-stressing the engines. In a more worrying context, SAC reported that 408 airmen, almost one percent of the complement, were absent without leave. Moreover, accident rates were very high, with 60 accidents for every 100,000 flying hours.

Responding to these deep concerns about the inadequate state of readiness displayed by SAC over the Berlin crisis, and to both political and Pentagon concerns about his leadership, on 19 October 1948 Kenney was replaced by Curtis LeMay and a week later Thomas D Power replaced McMullen, who was reassigned as commanding general of San Antonio Air Material area. Kenney was transferred to command of the Air University at Maxwell Field. LeMay would remain in command of SAC until 30 June 1957 when he was replaced by 'Tommy' Power, who would remain in command until 30 November 1964. Together, LeMay and Power would hone SAC into one of the most respected, and envied, combat commands in the history of US air power.

Securing Success

Immediately after receiving command of SAC, LeMay went to Andrews AFB outside Washington DC, where he discovered that there was not one crew that could 'do a professional job. Not one of the outfits was up to strength – neither in airplanes nor in people nor anything else'. LeMay's goal was clear, in that SAC 'had to be ready to go to war not next week, not tomorrow, but this afternoon, today...We had to operate every day as if we were at war', adding that he would not settle for anything less than a force 'so professional, so strong, so powerful, that we would not have to fight'.

The first job was to inspect SAC at its core – the bases and the crews which served its mission and the objectives. On 10 December 1948, LeMay visited Topeka AFB, Kansas, and was alarmed at the poor conditions, the inadequate mess facilities, poor location of fresh and waste food storage and the general lack of adequate accommodation for personnel. Unimpressed by explanations of uncooperative contractors assigned construction of better housing, three days later he visited Kearney AFB, Nebraska, and found the

The B-36 presented a revolution in capabilities although the Air Force struggled to come to grips with the gigantic behemoth and integrate its technical difficulties into operational schedules. (USAF)

same inadequate facilities for the married men and on 16 December he arrived at Carswell AFB, Texas, where the mighty B-36 entered operational service. There, LeMay suggested engagement with the local communities to give the local populace a sense of connection with the Air Force in general and with SAC in particular, calling for local builders to put up low-cost but comfortable accommodation.

On the preparation of food, LeMay suggested that the head cooks visit local hotels and see how they got return visits from customers, claiming that the food should be so good that personnel refrain from going to the local diners. Over the following months and years, LeMay would design barracks, draw up plans for effective and homely living quarters, set up hobby groups and places where families could worship together.

LeMay was aware that Carswell would be the core facility for introducing the B-36 and wanted efficient and highly trained personnel, instructing the base commander to brook no obstacle in getting support for that when required:

> When you run up against a stone wall and you have to have help from Eighth Air Force or SAC, start screaming. Don't be satisfied with mediocre performances from my staff people. All you have to worry about is fighting or getting ready to fight. Nothing makes me madder than staff officers and directives from Washington who pass it on instead of doing something about it themselves. If staff is passing work on to combat units they should be doing themselves, I want to know about it. If they are not helping they are not doing their job.

Despite 1948 being a challenging year, several notable flights took place in an attempt to demonstrate the range and long-duration capability of SAC's aircraft. On 29 July the 43rd BG sent three B-29s from Davis-Monthan on an attempted flight around the world. Planned to take 14 days, it was extended by a day when one aircraft crashed into the Arabian Sea. The circumnavigation was completed in 103 hours and 50 minutes flying time by the two remaining aircraft, one commanded by Lieutenant Colonel R W Kline and the other by 1st Lieutenant A M Neal, landing back at base on 6 August. Long-range flights such as this demonstrated a sustainable sequence of separate legs in different environmental conditions and across various locations.

To demonstrate the extreme range of the new aircraft then entering service, a B-36B of the 7th BG commanded by Major J D Bartlett set off across the Pacific Ocean from Carswell AFB, Texas, on 7 December, flying a distance of more than 8,000 miles (12,872km) non-stop to Hawaii in 35 hours and 30 minutes. Departing from Carswell on the same day, a B-50 from the 43rd BG made the same flight in 41 hours and 40 minutes, flying a more circuitous route of 9,870 miles (15,880km) receiving three inflight refuelling sessions from KB-29M tankers of the 43rd and 509th Air Refuelling Squadrons.

Despite challenges gearing up with new aircraft and problems with support for the Berlin airlift, SAC ran a bombing competition in 1948 with the intention of measuring both proficiency and accuracy, establishing mechanisms for competitiveness, quality and teamwork across the various participating units. There had been persistent concerns at the lack of necessary standards, where 3,000ft (914m) CEP (Circular Error Probable), where 50 percent of bombs dropped from 25,000ft (7,620m) will fall within that defined radius from the target. During 1947 crews had shown wide variations in performance, showing anything from 2,600ft (792m) to 4,000ft (1,219m).

This first was held at Castle AFB between 20 and 27 June 1948 when 10 groups took part, each providing three aircraft for the contest. Targets were set at the Wendover, Utah, bombing range

The B-36 required 12–15 crewmembers for each operational mission and a considerable increase in ground equipment and base installations, challenging the Air Force to expand its support infrastructure. (USAF)

with drops confined to 25,000ft (7,620m) consisting of three visual and three radar sightings for each release to the target. The Eighth AF got the top five places, achieving an average CEP of 2,000ft (610m) followed by the Fifteenth AF and the 307th BG. The best individual crew award went to 1st Lieutenant M J Jones of the 509th BG despite that group achieving a CEP of only 4,000ft (1,219m). But competitions were no way to improve standards, merely highlighting the status quo.

Concerned at the lack of accuracy in some of the unit scores, LeMay decided to extend the competitions to annual events, believing that the performance in the 1948 event had shown marked improvement, if only because of the challenge posed to each crew. LeMay strongly supported mechanisms to improve team spirit and to encourage competitiveness as a means of stimulating performance and pride. The second bombing competition was held 3–7 October 1949 and included 12 bomb groups, three with the B-36, seven with the B-29 and two with the B-50. Spurred on by their lack of placing in the 1948 competition, the Fifteenth AF succeeded in getting top honours, despite the 93rd BG switching to B-29s when the new B-50s it had sprung fuel leaks. The individual crew trophy went to a 28th BG B-36 crew.

After the 1949 bombing competition, LeMay introduced the spot-promotion programme where 237 commanders and crew members displaying outstanding contributions were raised from the grade of 1st lieutenant to a temporary grade of captain. This would be expanded in 1950 and 1951 to include the promotion to ranks of major, lieutenant colonel, technical sergeant and master sergeant and would be the hallmark of service in SAC. LeMay created the closest doctrine of a meritocracy in military ranks possible in the Air Force and stimulated a greatly enthused desire to achieve and to be seen to exceed job requirements by gaining credit for outstanding performance. But it worked the other way; a slacking of that standard would result in the spot promotions being taken away, for the individual and for the entire crew.

The annual bombing competitions would be a test of integrated teamwork and the proficiency of individual squadrons as reflected through the training and experience obtained by each bomber crew. A lot of the training involved rehearsals through radar bomb scoring, which had its genesis in the Second World War. Introduced initially by the British, night bombing by radar was forced upon the RAF by operations calling for crews to gain accuracy on designated targets in the dark and in poor weather. Over Europe that was most of the time and while the British had the designs for this equipment shared with the United States, it was American research and engineering that honed the equipment to an advanced level, utilised by both allies.

Radar Bomb Scoring (RBS) activity for SAC originated through the 206th Army Air Force Base Unit (AAFBU) activated at Colorado Springs on 6 June 1945 under the command of Colonel Robert W Burns. It had two SCR-584 radar detachments at Kansas City and Fort Worth, Texas, and additional detachments were set up at Denver, Colorado, Chicago, Illinois, Omaha, Nebraska, Albuquerque, New Mexico, and Los Angeles, California. This unit was re-designated the 63rd AAFBU on 24 July 1945 under the Continental Air Forces but on 5 March 1946 it moved back to Colorado Springs and re-designated the 263rd AAFBU three days later.

Under SAC it was moved from assignment with the Fifteenth AF to the Headquarters SAC where it grew its capabilities. The number of RBS runs was relatively low at first, with only 880 in

Operating costs and funding requirements were a serious constraint on expansion for an air force already constrained by government cuts in budgets, men and materiel. (USAF)

1946, increasing to 2,499 in 1947 but under LeMay that activity was stepped up and considerable emphasis placed on giving crews a far higher exposure to simulated attacks and bomb runs. In 1948 there were 12,084 runs and this would increase to a peak of 28,049. On 21 July 1948, the unit was re-designated the 3903rd Radar Bomb Scoring Squadron and on 19 January 1951 it would be upgraded from a Squadron to a Group with 12 detachments and three bomb reporting squadrons.

Bombing accuracy was key to a successful mission in real-world situations and LeMay was concerned at the poor record demonstrated to date. In January 1949 a simulated radar bombing mission was conducted against Dayton, Ohio, in which only 71 out of 101 B-29s assigned actually left the ground. Only 303 bombing runs were completed at an altitude of 30,000ft (9,100m) rather than the usual 10,000–15,000ft (3,048–4,572m), two-thirds getting no closer to their targets than 10,090ft (3,075m). Aiming had been seriously compromised by the freezing conditions, heavy rain and thick cloud.

Frustrated, LeMay remarked that not one aircraft had completed its planned mission. Had this been the miss distance over Hiroshima or Nagasaki, the target cities would have been left unscathed. The blast wave and fireball of a Mk III implosion-type atom bomb was insufficient to achieve desired results should the detonation distance be greater than 2,000ft (610m) from the target. While much had been made by the public and the press in general about the destructive potential of fission bombs, in reality they were not as destructive as had been assumed and the ability of a SAC bomber to get within 1,000ft (305m) was a requirement, given the type of material against which the bomb would be detonated.

It was for this reason that after it became known that the USSR had its own bomb there was pressure from expert opinion that the limitations of the fission bomb were too constraining for the role envisaged. That, and the need to ensure total destruction in difficult circumstances against targets which could be obscured convinced the Truman administration that development of the 'super', a fission, or 'hydrogen' bomb was warranted. The implications of that for SAC will be explored in *Volume 5: Bombers 1950–1953*.

The threat posed by the Soviet bomb ran deep, challenging the confidence in military superiority which the Truman administration had believed it had bestowed upon the American public. The shock news made headlines and politicians wanted answers. There were delicate issues in the reaction to this news and in a highly classified letter to Vandenberg, on 12 December 1949, LeMay debated the value of a pre-emptive or preventative war, a first strike on the Soviet Union to destroy its warfighting capability before it could be deployed. Citing a need to follow what he perceived to be Vandenberg's position, LeMay 'stressed the importance of accelerating our readiness to conduct effective atomic warfare'.

LeMay also worried about what he perceived to be the threat of a Soviet first-strike, given 'the information available to us', adding the chilling thought that 'it is unlikely that we can prevent the Soviets from attaining a measure of success in any attacks against our striking force…we have little or no margin of safety'. Moreover, he asserted, 'it would appear economical and logical to adopt the objective of completely avoiding enemy attack against our strategic force by destroying his atomic force before it can attack ours'.

It has never been declassified but the views expressed by Vandenberg and the degree to which LeMay acquiesced, or indeed initiated the discussion regarding a pre-emptive strike to neutralise Soviet war-making capabilities is not currently known. Under LeMay, the entire structure of SAC would be orientated toward a deterrent force capable of meeting warmongering assertions from the Soviet Union. His disclosed response to Vandenberg is illuminating, in that it presupposes the validity of the premise while shaping it to the laws of war and the belief in political circles that the United States should not initiate a conflict through first-strike or pre-emptive means:

> Assuming that as a democracy we are not prepared to wage a preventive war, this course of action poses two most difficult requirements: (1) An intelligence system which can locate the vulnerable elements of the Soviet striking force and forewarn us when attack by that force is imminent, and (2) Agreement at top governmental level that when such information is received the Strategic Air Command will be directed to attack.

It strikes a fine line between belief and certain knowledge, proposing that the United States should be prepared to go to war if it became unequivocally convinced that Russia was about to attack and that this would be sufficient to afford legal sanction and moral justification on the basis that it would save lives and shorten the period of armed action. It was on this cusp of interpretation as to enemy intentions that the preparedness of SAC for war at any hour was raised to the minimum level that LeMay would accept for alert and readiness conditions. It was this that drove his policies in commanding SAC and not the unabashed aggression with which he has been accused.

These exchanges and the letter of 12 December 1949 is the reason why LeMay placed considerable emphasis on the reconnaissance role and why he pushed hard for such a mission attached to the incoming B-36 and the B-47, while maintaining a strong data-gathering role for both photographic and signals intelligence-gathering missions on the border with, and at times inside, the Soviet Union and its occupied territories. In that he would find common ground with Dwight D Eisenhower when serving as President from January 1953 to January 1961, the most 'intelligence-orientated' occupant of the White House in history.

Deputy Commander at SAC until he replaced LeMay in 1957, Thomas Power was no less controversial than his boss and interpretations as to his character are influenced greatly by the subjective opinion of the observer. Power had been airborne commander for the air flotilla at Bikini Atoll for Operation CROSSROADS and witnessed the atomic tests, observing that it 'made an even greater impression on me, compared with the previous bombings I had seen'. With LeMay at the XXIst, Power had been closely involved in planning the low-level B-29 raids on Japanese cities in 1945 and was crucial to that policy being implemented. He had great experience of strategic bombing and originated many of the flight operations carried out by the bomber crews.

Called back from Europe, where he had been planning the bases for B-29s at the beginning of the Berlin airlift, Power was tasked by LeMay with completely transforming the way SAC was run and the standards required of its personnel. Hewitt Whelass, Power's deputy, believed that 'LeMay had the reputation, but Power was the toughest guy I ever knew because when he said something be done in a certain way once a decision was made, he made sure you did it', adding that if someone 'disagreed 100 percent with the boss he could speak his piece', but when he was ordered to carry out the task 'there was no compromise...he was that tough a guy...many Wing Commanders were fired because they didn't carry it out the way it was supposed to be, and that was Power'.

Some outsiders charged Power with being 'sadistic' and when asked if he believed that was so, LeMay concurred: 'He was. He was sort of an aristocratic bastard...but he got things done'. Convinced that human performance was related to personal health, Power put judo as a central part of fitness, encouraging enlisted men to go to Japan to fully understand how it should be done and personally learned judo from Emilio Bruno who did so much to bring the art to America. Later, Power would seek to intimidate dissenting officers by challenging them to a bout on the judo mat!

The period 1948–1949 brought many changes to SAC, to its equipment, aircraft, personnel and the command structure. But amid the transformation from an unprepared and sometimes dysfunctional organisation some progress was achieved and that provided a solid start on a very new way of managing and operating the nation's strategic strike force. Fortunately, these changes were taking effect just before SAC was challenged to set up and commit resources to the demands of the Korean War which would shock the world when North Korea invaded South Korea in June 1950.

In 1949 the year began with intensive training of B-29 and B-50 crews and as part of the improvements to crew operations in bombing tests and simulated attacks, a Lead Crew School was set up at Walker AFB, New Mexico. This was already showing improvements over the previous year. In addition, to give crews the experience of living and working overseas, selected bases hosted personnel on rotation from the United States. The stress of these activities intentionally placed crews in a pseudo combat environment and the persistent problem with housing and general facilities at numerous places around the world posed problems. However, 50 percent of those discharged at the end of their term of service returned to fill their vacated slots. This was more than many commanders expected but far less than had been hoped for.

Keen to stretch the global wings of its new and potent B-50A, an aircraft from the 43rd BG (46-010. "*Lucky Lady II*") completed a flight around the world on 2 March, logging 23,452 miles (37,734km) in 94 hours and 1 minute carrying a crew of 14 commanded by Captain J Gallagher from Carswell AFB. The aircraft had been refuelled in the air four times by KB-29 tankers of the 43rd Air Refuelling Squadron. The achievement raised publicity and numerous awards for the crew and the event itself won the Mackay Trophy for 1949, awarded each year by the National Aeronautic Association for a feat of outstanding national accomplishment. Great expectations had been placed on the B-50 and the Air Force was keen to use it as a symbol of their new assets and to serve as a recruiting tool.

Just 10 days after the B-50 returned, a B-36 of the 7th BG arrived back at its home base of Fort Worth, Texas, having flown 9,600 miles (15,446km) in 43 hours and 7 minutes without refuelling. It had been flown by a crew of 12 commanded by Captain Roy Showalter. This flight was one of many being conducted to evaluate the performance of this new behemoth, providing vital information on speed, high-altitude performance and weight carrying capacity as well as to assess the effectiveness of the comprehensive air armament and to conduct simulated penetration of enemy defences. A giant in its class, the B-36 had tremendous potential but enormous challenges due to its sheer size, the number and type of pusher-engines it had and the amount of time required to service and maintain it.

On 6 April 1949 the 3rd Air Division came under the jurisdiction of SAC for its rotational duties to the UK and its commanding general, Major General Leon W Johnson, reported directly to headquarters USAF and to LeMay. On 1 November, the Second AF

A new age of jet-powered aircraft brought unprecedented demand for specialist technical skills supported by a wide-ranging education and training programme for aircrew and ground technicians. (USAF)

Built as a B-50D, 48-096 was seconded to NACA where it was converted into a mothership for carrying the Bell X-2, a rocket-powered research programme, and the replacement for a B-50A (46-0011) which had an accident. (NACA)

was activated at Barksdale AFB, Louisiana, and assigned to SAC Headquarters with personnel from the 311th Air Division relocated from Forbes AFB, Kansas, when that unit was disbanded. Six days later, the Fifteenth AF headquarters moved from Ent AFB, Colorado, to March AFB, California.

The year saw a major transition in aircraft types, the paper returns showing 868 tactical aircraft of which there were 390 B-29s, 62 RB-29s, 67 KB-29s, 99 B-50s and 36 B-36s. Three heavy bomb groups were equipping with the B-36 and 11 medium bomber groups operated the B-29 and the B-50, while two fighter groups had the F-86 and the F-82. Three reconnaissance groups had RB-29s, 18 RB-17s and C-82s and two strategic support squadrons had C-54s and YC-97s while six air refuelling squadrons operated the KB-29s in their new role. In all, during 1949 SAC had 17 bases in the United States. Overall, SAC had 71,490 officers, airmen and civilians, up more than one-third on 1948.

A Note on Historical Sources

The source material for these volumes originates from primary references and peer-reviewed historical reports and analyses which, over the ensuing decades since the events from which they were compiled took place, have been re-examined with the additional advantage of access to declassified material and further investigation.

Here, a concerted effort has been made not to use the work of aviation writers past or present for reference. The vast majority of recognised aviation and aeronautical historians provide valued material in books or articles and their work can be a useful resource for the armchair enthusiast and active hobbyist as well as for the professional historian. Moreover, there are now many specialised internet-based resources embracing special-interest-groups (SIGs) to encourage further exchange of information.

However, a very few writers, usually known within the fraternity of aviation historians and pressured by deadlines and delivery dates, use regurgitated text which can be flawed or too generalised to warrant credible repetition. In almost all instances, verification is key to establishing fact from speculation or assumption and that can be a time-consuming activity which demand high levels of commitment.

In studying the history of US air power, a general and readily accessible resource is the *Air Force Historical Foundation* which has a peer-reviewed journal issued four times each year with numerous articles and special features directing attention to specific events, theatres of engagement or equipment. It is a valued and highly respected source for initial contact with events and activities throughout the period covered by these volumes.

Also of great use is the Air University at Maxwell AFB, Alabama, and the Air University Press, which is the academic publisher of the US Air Force. Together, their publicly available materials have provided the author with reliable and verified information. In addition, the US Department of Defense, the Air Force Historical Support Division, the Historical Office of the Secretary of Defense, the Naval History and Heritage Command and the US National Archives were visited and consulted during a professional association over many decades. Collectively, they have provided material from which these volumes are compiled.

On the recording of inventories, it is noted that individual units and commands were not always accurate in the numbers of aircraft claimed to be on strength and in some cases there were attempts to raise quotas artificially, little discrimination being made as to aircraft assigned versus those operationally available, factors which vary day by day. There are also variations in performance figures quoted

General Omar Bradley became the first Chairman of the Joint Chiefs of Staff (CJCS) on 19 August 1949, a distinguished and influential job which would be the highest, uniformed position in the Department of Defense. (JCS)

in numerous official reports for specific types of aircraft. Aircraft performance is much argued over by amateur and professional historians.

To be specific for instance, there is no 'maximum speed' for a particular aircraft type, except that defined as an engineering or atmospheric limit on structural stress or capability. Speed varies according to load, altitude, fuel levels and variations in engine performance, all variables which skew the recorded values. In these volumes, the USAF Standard Aircraft Characteristics charts have been used to show the equivalent values for realistic comparison between types but here too there are variations which affect performance levels of individual aircraft.

Supplementing military histories and the various official unit command diaries are manufacturers' logs and production records. Here, the annual yearbooks of *The Aircraft Industries Association of America* for the chronological periods in question proved invaluable for obtaining annual data from which has been drawn production numbers and various engineering developments and achievements. The individual manufacturers also provided archival material from which events and activities were reconstructed.

For specific contextual alignment between events and the period within which they occurred, an invaluable asset is the digitisation of every issue of *Aviation Week*, the aviation trade journal for which every issue since it was first published in 1916 is available for subscribers to their platform. It is within such coverage that transient and inconsequential events and activities can add perspective or context.

This C-97G was converted from a KC-97G back to an all-cargo variant, frequently utilised on MATS routes across the United States. (Alan Radecki)

Other periodicals and journals are less readily available in print form but if they can be found they are frequently a valuable resource for detailed accounts of little-known events. One valued and highly accessible organisation is the *American Aviation Historical Society*. It publishes a journal which covers both civil and military US aviation from its earliest days to the recent past and frequently records the experiences of individuals and organisations. Digital subscribers can access every issue for reference.

The content of the *US Air Power 1945–1990* series comes from all of the above and the author's files compiled through access to numerous organisations, government departments, company archives, learned societies and academic institutions across 60 years of professional involvement, with the help and assistance of individuals and respected aviation historians around the world. All of which to whom the author is indebted.

BIBLIOGRAPHY

Anderson, F, *Northrop, An Aeronautical History* (Century City, California: Northrop Corporation, 1976)

Andrade, J. M., *U.S. Military Designations and Serials 1909-1979* (Midland Countries Publications, 1997)

Avery, N., *North American Aircraft 1934-1998 Volume I* (Santa Ana, California: Narkiewicz/ Thompson, 1998)

Baker, David, *Convair B-36 Peacemaker* (Sparkford: Haynes Publishing, 2020)

Baker, David, *Convair B-36 Peacemaker* (Stamford: Key Publishing, 2024)

Barlow, Jeffrey G., *Revolt of the Admirals: The Fight for Naval Aviation 1945-1950* (Washington DC: Naval Historical Center, Department of the Navy, 1994)

Bauer, E. E., *Boeing in Peace and War* (Enumclaw, Washington: TABA Publishing, 1990)

Bilstein, R. E., *Orders of Magnitude, A History of the NACA and NASA 1915-1990* SP-4406 (Washington DC: National Aeronautics and Space Administration, 1989)

Bowers, Peter M., *Boeing Aircraft since 1916* (London: Putnam Aeronautical Books, 1989)

Breihan, J. R., Piet, S., Mason R. S., *Martin Aircraft 1909-1960* (Santa Ana, California: Narkiewicz/Thompson, 1998)

Bridgman, L (ed), *Jane's All the World Aircraft 1948-49* (Jane's Publishing, 1948); *Jane's All the World's Aircraft 1949-50* (Jane's Publishing, 1949)

Bright, Charles D., *The Jet Makers: The Aerospace Industry from 1945 to 1972* (Lawrence: The Regents Press of Kansas, 1978)

Brown, Shannon A., (ed), *Providing the Means of War: Perspectives on Defense Acquisition, 1945-2000* (Washington DC: US Army Center of Military History and Industrial College of the Armed Forces, 2005)

Buttler, Tony, *American Secret Projects: Fighters and Interceptors 1945-1976* (Hinckley: Midland Publishing, 2007)
Converse, Elliott V., III, *Rearming for the Cold War 1945-1960* (Washington DC: Historical Office, Office of the Secretary of Defense, 2012)
Daso, Dik A., *Architects of Air Supremacy: General Hap Arnold and Dr. Theodore von Karman* (Maxwell, Alaska: Air University Press, 1997)
Dawson, V. P., *Engines and Innovation: Lewis Laboratory and American Propulsion Technology* (Atglen, Pennsylvania: Schiffer Publishing, 1991)
Francillon, Rene J., *Lockheed Aircraft since 1913* (London: Putnam & Company, 1982)
Francillon, Rene J., *McDonnell Douglas Aircraft since 1920* (London: Putnam & Company, 1979)
Frisbee, John L., *Makers of the United States Air Force* (Washington DC: Air Force History and Museums Program, 1996)
Goldberg, Alfred, *A History of the United States Air Force* (Washington DC: Arno Press, 1957)
Hansen, J. R., *Engineer in Charge, A History of the Langley Aeronautical Laboratory 1917-1958* SP-4305 (Washington DC: National Aeronautics and Space Administration, 1987)
Hartman, E. P., *Adventures in Research, A History of Ames Research Center 1940-1965* SP-4302 (Washington DC, National Aeronautics and Space Administration, 1970)
Holley, Irving Brinton Jr., *Buying Aircraft: Materiel Procurement for the Army Air Forces* (Washington DC: Center of Military History, United States Army, 1989)
Jenkins, D. R., and Landis, T. R., *Magnesium Overcast, The Story of the Convair B-36* (Hinckley: Specialty Press, 2001)
Johnson, Stephen B., *The United States Air Force and the Culture of Innovation, 1945-1965* (Washington DC: United States Air Force History and Museums Program, 2002)
Kaplan, Fred, *The Wizards of Armageddon* (Standford, California: Touchstone, 1983)
Kay, A. L., *Turbojet, History & Development 1930-1960 Volume 2* (Ramsbury: Crowood Press, 2007)
Knaack, M. S., *Encyclopedia of US Air Force Aircraft and Missile Systems Volume 2: Post-World War II Bombers 1945-1973* (Washington DC: Office of Air Force History, 1978)
Lloyd, Alwyn T., *Boeing's B-47 Stratojet* (Hinckley: Specialty Press, 2005)
Loftin, L. F., Jr., *Quest for Performance, The Evolution of Modern Aircraft*, SP-468 (Washington DC, National Aeronautics and Space Administration, 1985)
Moody, Walton S., *Building a Strategic Air Force* (Washington DC: United States Air Force and Museums Program, 1996)
Nagle, James F., *A History of Government Contracting* (Washington DC: George Washington University, 1999)
Neufeld, J. (*ed*), *Research and Development in the United States Air Force* (Washington DC: Center for Air Force History, United States Air Force, 1993)
Neufeld, J., Watson, G. M. Jr., and Chenoweth, D. (ed), *Technology and the Air Force, a Retrospective Assessment* (Washington DC: Air Force History and Museums Program, 1997)
Norton, Bill, *American Aircraft Development: World War Two Legacy 1945-1953 and The Korean War* (Stroud: Fonthill Media Ltd, 2001)
Patillo, Donald M., *Pushing the Envelope: The American Aircraft Industry* (Ann Arbor: The University of Michigan Press, 1998)
Polmar, Norman, *Strategic Air Command* (Cambridge: Patrick Stephens, 1979)
Pyeatt, Don, and Jenkins, Dennis R., *Cold War Peacemaker* (Hinckley: Speciality Press, 2010)
Rae, John B., *Climb to Greatness: The American Aircraft Industry 1920-1960* (Cambridge, Mass.: The MIT Press, 1968)
Sturm, Thomas A., *The USAF Scientific Advisory Board: The first Twenty Years 1944-1964* (Washington DC: USAF Historical Division Liaison Office, 1967)
Swanborough G., and Bowers, P. M., *United States Military Aircraft since 1909* (London: Putnam Aeronautical Books, 1989)
White, Graham, *R-2800 Pratt & Whitney's Dependable Masterpiece* (Shrewsbury: Airlife Publishing Ltd, 2001)
White, Graham, *R-4360 Pratt & Whitney's Major Miracle* (Hinckley: Specialty Press, 2006)
Wolk, Herman S., *The Struggle of Air Force Independence, 1943-1947* (Washington DC: United States Air Force History and Museums Program, 1997)

About the Author

Born to an RAF family in England toward the end of the Second World War, the author has had a professional career within aerospace, working with NASA, the US Air Force and aviation manufacturers before becoming a professional aerospace historian and writer. Elected to the International Academy of Astronautics, David has also received: the Rolls-Royce Award for the Best Propulsion Submission, RAeS Aerospace Journalist of the Year Awards 1998; the Arthur C Clarke Award (2005); and the American Astronautical Society's Frederick I Ordway Award (2017) presented at the NASA Marshall Space Flight Center. During the 1980s, David was managing director of his aerospace consulting company with offices in London and Princeton, New Jersey. He has been editor of *Horizons*, the house magazine of the former Smith's Industries, two Jane's yearbooks, *Aviation News* and *SpaceFlight* magazine. Apart from aerospace, David is interested in geopolitics, the history of twentieth century warfare, film and classical music, when he is not engaging with the natural world with his wife Ann.